THE TROUBLE WITH

NORMAL

MICHAEL WARNER

THE TROUBLE WITH

NORMAL

SEX, POLITICS, AND THE
ETHICS OF QUEER LIFE

HARVARD UNIVERSITY PRESS

CAMBRIDGE, MASSACHUSETTS

First Harvard University Press paperback edition, 2000
Originally published by The Free Press

Text design and composition by Ellen R. Sasahara

Library of Congress Cataloging-in-Publication Data
Warner, Michael
The Trouble with normal : sex, politics, and the ethics of queer
life / Michael Warner.
p.   cm.
1. Sexual ethics. 2. Homosexuality. 3. Gays. I. Title.
HQ32.W367   1999   99-44356
CIP
ISBN 0-674-00441-8 (pbk.)

CONTENTS

PREFACE

This book rises from the abstract to the concrete. It opens with general questions of ethics and moves to very local politics. In the later chapters, when it gets down to business, so to speak, it makes arguments that many will view as extremist, if not insane. For example, I argue that marriage is unethical. At a time when the largest gay organizations are pushing for same-sex marriage, I argue that this strategy is a mistake and that it represents a widespread loss of vision in the movement. In the fourth chapter, I go so far as to offer a principled defense of pornography, sex businesses, and sex outside the home.

Partly in order to convince the reader that I am not simply unhinged, I begin the book on a rather different note. The first chapter lays out a set of ethical principles that I take to be fundamental to political disputes around sex. It sets out an ideal of sexual autonomy and tries to imagine the conditions under which that ideal could be met. It points to a number of ways that the politics of sexual shame makes that ideal impossible for variant sexualities. And it suggests that queer culture has long cultivated an alternative ethical culture that is almost never recognized by mainstream moralists as anything of the kind. I believe that the ethical insights of this sexual culture provide the best explanation of the political controversies that I later address in subsequent chapters: first, the increasingly popular call for gay people to see themselves as normal Americans; then, the campaign for same-sex marriage that has been the principal rallying point of the normalizing movement; followed by a chapter on the local politics of sex in New York City, where I live.

The analysis laid out in the opening of the book could also apply to many other examples. Although the work generally deals with conflicts in gay politics—not surprisingly, considering that my theme is the politics of sexual shame, and considering that local activism was the context that prompted me to write it—this subject involves a great deal more than the politics of the gay and lesbian movement, conventionally considered. Indeed, one of my contentions is that the movement has defined itself too narrowly. After the Clinton impeachment, nothing can be clearer than the degree to which a politics of sexual shame and conflicts over sex can be found across the full spectrum of contemporary life. From daily jostlings in home and workplace to the spectacular crises of national media politics, sex roils people; and the usual idea of what would be an ethical response is a moralism that roils them more. For this reason the world has much to learn from the disreputable queers who have the most experience in the politics of shame, but who for that very reason have been least likely to gain a hearing—either in the official policy circles where their interests are allegedly represented or in the theoretical and philosophical debates about morality, sex, and shame where their point of view can be most transformative. Articulating that point of view in a way that people can hear is not always easy. I imagine everyone has had the experience of moving abruptly from one context to another and finding that a tone or an idea that worked in the first looks absurd or improper in the second. You could be gossiping in a corner and suddenly realize that everyone in the room is listening. You could be practicing a formal speech at home only to discover that it sounds pompous or corny. Finding the right thing to say can be of little use unless one can find the right register in which to say it. The gulf that this book tries to bridge is unusually wide. It explains why those who care about policy and morality should take as their point of departure the perspective of those at the bottom of the scale of respectability: queers, sluts, prostitutes, trannies, club crawlers, and other lowlifes. And it urges, for these people, a politics consistent with what I take to be their best traditions. If the result is a wavering register, a bit of growl in the falsetto, the indulgent reader will chalk it up to the nature of the problem that I have set out to address, and the peculiar kind of drag it requires.

CHAPTER ONE

THE ETHICS OF SEXUAL SHAME

Sooner or later, happily or unhappily, almost everyone fails to control his or her sex life. Perhaps as compensation, almost everyone sooner or later also succumbs to the temptation to control *someone else's* sex life. Most people cannot quite rid themselves of the sense that controlling the sex of others, far from being unethical, is where morality begins. Shouldn't it be possible to allow everyone sexual autonomy, in a way consistent with everyone else's sexual autonomy? As simple as this ethical principle sounds, we have not come close to putting it into practice. The culture has thousands of ways for people to govern the sex of others—and not just harmful or coercive sex, like rape, but the most personal dimensions of pleasure, identity, and practice. We do this directly, through prohibition and regulation, and indirectly, by embracing one identity or one set of tastes as though they were universally shared, or should be. Not only do we do this; we congratulate ourselves for doing it. To do otherwise would require us to rethink much of what passes as common sense and morality.

It might as well be admitted that sex is a disgrace. We like to say nicer things about it: that it is an expression of love, or a noble endowment of the Creator, or liberatory pleasure. But the possibility of abject shame is never entirely out of the picture. If the camera doesn't cut away at the right moment, or if the door is thrown open unwontedly, or the walls turn out to be too thin, all the fine dress of piety and pride will be found tangled around one's ankles. In the fourth century B.C., the Athenian philosopher Diogenes thought that the sense of shame was hypocrisy, a denial of our appetitive nature, and he found a simple way to dramatize the problem: he masturbated in the marketplace. Many centuries of civilization have passed since then, but this example is not yet widely followed.

An ethical response to the problem of shame should not require us to pretend that shame doesn't exist. That, essentially, is what Diogenes wanted to do. Most defenders of sexual freedom still try some version of this response. They say that sexuality should be valued as pleasurable and life-affirming; or, some say, as a kind of spirituality. Still others see sex as a radical subversion of repressive power. Whatever truth may lie in these or similar ideas about why sex is good, I suspect that most people sense a certain hollowness to these anodyne views of sexuality as simply benign and pleasant. People know better, though they may not admit it. As Leo Bersani wrote in a classic essay of 1987, "There is a big secret about sex: most people don't like it." Perhaps because sex is an occasion for losing control, for merging one's consciousness with the lower orders of animal desire and sensation, for raw confrontations of power and demand, it fills people with aversion and shame. Opponents of moralism, in Bersani's view, have too often painted a sanitized, pastoral picture of sex, as though it were simply joy, light, healing, and oneness with the universe. Many of the moralists do the same when they pretend that sex is or should be only about love and intimacy. Either way, these descriptions of affirmative sex begin to sound anything but sexy. And no matter how true they might be, at least for some people, it is futile to deny the ordinary power of sexual shame.

So the difficult question is not: how do we get rid of sexual shame? The answer to that one will inevitably be: get rid of sex. The question, rather, is this: what will we do with our shame? And the usual response is: pin it on someone else. Sexual shame is not just a fact of life; it is also political. Although nearly everyone can be easily embarrassed about sex, some people stand at greater risk than others. They might be beaten, murdered, jailed, or merely humiliated. They might be stigmatized as deviants or criminals. They might even be impeached. More commonly, they might simply be rendered inarticulate, or frustrated, since shame makes some pleasures tacitly inadmissable, unthinkable. They might find themselves burdened by furtiveness, or by extraordinary needs for disclosure, or by such a fundamental need to wrench free from the obvious that the idea of an alternative is only the dim anticipation of an unformed wish. In any case, they will find it hard to distinguish their shame from its politics, their personal failings from the power of alien norms.

For most people, at least, the ethical response to sexual shame seems to be: more shame. The unethical nature of this response jumps out when we consider the moralisms of the past. The early-eighteenth-century tract *Onania*, for example, declares that masturbation is a sin "that perverts and extinguishes nature: he who is guilty of it, is laboring at the Destruction of his Kind, and in a manner strikes at the Creation itself." Reading this tortured logic, it's easy to wonder: what were they thinking? More important: why were they so driven to control something that we now recognize as harmless, and by definition not our business? To most readers, I suspect, the irrationality of past moralisms is reassuring: we're smarter than that now. But it could just as easily alarm us, since pronouncements about what kind of sex is or isn't good for others are by no means a thing of the past. Religious groups no longer say much about God's punishment of Onan for masturbation, but they still invoke biblical authority against gay people, sadomasochists, fetishists, and other alleged sex offenders. The secular arguments persist as well: though few people still think that the preservation of the species is a law of nature that has to be executed in every orgasm, they do still think that marital hetero sex has a rationale in nature, however Darwinian, and that it is therefore normative. These alibis of sexual morality crop up everywhere, from common prejudice to academic psychology. Popularized versions of evolutionary biology are enjoying quite a vogue now because they seem to justify the status quo as an expression of natural law.

Perhaps we should call it moralism, rather than morality, when some sexual tastes or practices (or rather an idealized version of them) are mandated for everyone. All too commonly, people think not only that their own way of living is right, but that it should be everyone else's moral standard as well. They don't imagine that sexual variance can be consistent with morality. And they think that anyone who disagrees with their version of morality must be a fuzzy relativist. Their suspicion of sexual variance is pseudo-morality, the opposite of an ethical respect for the autonomy of others. To say this is not to reject all morality, as some conservatives would have us believe; it is itself a moral argument. After all, it would be hard to constrain violence toward women, sissies, and variant sexualities if we thought that all morality were merely a version of the same coercion. Some shame may be well deserved. The difficulty is that moralism is so easily mistaken for morality. Some kinds of sexual relations seem as though they ought to be universal. They seem innocently moral, consistent with nature and health. But what if they are not universal in fact, or if other people demonstrate a different understanding of nature and health? It would take an extraordinary effort to consider the views of these sexual dissidents with anything like openness, because the first instinct will be to think of them as immoral, criminal, or pathological. And of course they might be. But anytime it seems necessary to explain away other people's sex in these ways, the premises of one's morality could just be flawed. What looks like crime might be harmless difference. What looks like immorality might be a rival morality. What looks like pathology might be a rival form of health, or a higher tolerance of stress.

It would be nice if the burden of proof, in such questions of sexual morality, lay on those who want to impose their standard on someone else. Then the goal of sexual ethics would be to constrain coercion rather than shut down sexual variance. But things usually work the other way around. We do not begin with what the sports-minded like to call a level playing field. We live with sexual norms that survive from the Stone Age, including prohibitions against autoeroticism, sodomy, extramarital sex, and (for those who still take the Vatican seriously) birth control. This is a problem with any essentially conservative or traditionalist stance on sexual morality: what we have to conserve is barbaric. What we inherit from the past, in the realm of sex, is the morality of patriarchs and clansmen, souped up with Christian hostility to the flesh ("our vile body," Saint Paul called it), medieval chastity cults, virgin/whore complexes, and other detritus of ancient repression. Given these legacies of unequal moralism, nearly every civilized aspect of sexual morality has initially looked deviant, decadent, or sinful, including voluntary marriage, divorce, and nonreproductive sex. For many people, the antiquity of sexual norms is a reason to obey them. In *Bowers v. Hardwick* (1986), for example, the Supreme Court invoked the "ancient roots" of the prohibition against sodomy. Chief Justice Warren Burger noted that "decisions of individuals relating to homosexual conduct have been subject to state intervention throughout the history of Western civilization." One might have thought that such a hoary pedigree of barbarism was all the more reason for skepticism, but of course that wasn't Burger's conclusion.

When a given sexual norm has such deep layers of sediment, or blankets enough territory to seem universal, the effort of wriggling out from under it can be enormous. The burden becomes even heavier when one must first overcome shame, or break with the tacit force of a sexual morality that other people take to be obvious. We might even say that when sexual norms are of very great antiquity or generality, as the prohibition against sodomy has been until recently and still is for many people, they are hardly intended as coercion. No one has to try to dominate others through them. They are just taken for granted, scarcely entering consciousness at all. The world was homophobic, for example, before it identified any homosexuals for it to be phobic about. The unthinkability of sodomy may just be cultural landfill, rather than an insidious plan concocted by some genius of heterosexual world domination. Yet the effect is the same: heterosexual world domination. In fact, the effect is worse, because anyone who might have an interest in sodomy won't simply have to fight a known enemy, or overturn the prohibitions of the judges. He (or she, in some states) will first have to struggle with the unthinkability of his or her own desire. When battles have no enemies in this way, victories are rare.

The politics of shame, in other words, includes vastly more than the overt and deliberate shaming produced by moralists. It also involves silent inequalities, unintended effects of isolation, and the lack of public access. So sexual autonomy requires more than freedom of choice, tolerance, and the liberalization of sex laws. It requires access to pleasures and possibilities, since people commonly do not know their desires until they find them. Having an ethics of sex, therefore, does not mean having a theory about what people's desires are or should be. If the goal is sexual autonomy, consistent with everyone else's sexual autonomy, then it will be impossible to say in advance what form that will take. Even bondage can be a means of autonomy—or not. Moralism cannot; it can only produce complacent satisfaction in others' shame. The taken-for-grantedness of dominant sexuality has the same effect, as does the privatization or isolation of sexual experience.

For some gay men and lesbians, the alternative to the cramping effects of shame in our culture is to "celebrate diversity." I must confess that whenever I see this slogan I think: why? It sounds like a slogan for a shopping mall. Diversity might or might not be a good thing, depending on context. Culture requires common references and norms, as the slogan itself reveals by telling us all to celebrate the same thing. But in the case of sexual norms, it makes sense. Individuals do not go shopping for sexual identity, but they do have a stake in a culture that enables sexual variance and circulates knowledge about it, because they have no other way of knowing what they might or might not want, or what they might become, or with whom they might find a common lot.

Edith Wharton tells a story of asking her mother, just before her marriage, what to expect on her wedding night. She was told not to ask such a stupid question. "You've seen statues," her mother said. We call this Victorian repression, but what it repressed was something that Wharton only came to desire much later. The term "repression" is often applied retrospectively in this way. There is a catch-22 of sexual shame: you don't think of yourself as repressed until after you've made a break with repression. We forget that even very standard sexualities—in this case, matrimonial heterosexuality—require not just free choice but the public accessibility of sexual knowledge, ideally in a more useful form than statues.

Women and gay people have been especially vulnerable to the shaming effects of isolation. Almost all children grow up in families that think of themselves and all their members as heterosexual, and for some children this produces a profound and nameless estrangement, a sense of inner secrets and hidden shame. No amount of adult "acceptance" or progress in civil rights is likely to eliminate this experience of queerness for many children and adolescents. Later in life, they will be told that they are "closeted," as though they have been telling lies. They bear a special burden of disclosure. No wonder so much of gay culture seems marked by a primal encounter with shame, from the dramas of sadomasochism to the rhetoric of gay pride, or the newer "queer" politics. Ironically, plenty of moralists will then point to this theme of shame in gay life as though it were proof of something pathological in gay people. It seldom occurs to anyone that the dominant culture and its family environment should be held accountable for creating the inequalities of access and recognition that produce this sense of shame in the first place.

Most people, I hope, have had the experience of discovering deep pleasure in something they would not have said previously that they wanted. Yet the prevalent wisdom, oddly enough, seems to be that variant desires are legitimate only if they can be shown to be immutable, natural, and innate. If that were true, then statues would be enough. People wouldn't need an accessible culture of sex to tell them anything they deserved to know. Then again, it would be hard to justify *any* kind of sexuality on these grounds. It would be hard, for example, to justify the morality of marriage by finding a gene for it; it is a conventional legal relation. Because moralism so often targets not just sex but knowledge about sex, people come to believe, nonsensically, that moral or legitimate sex must be unlearned, prereflective, present before history, isolated from the public circulation of culture.

This is one reason why so many gay people are now desperately hoping that a gay gene can be found. They think they would be more justified if they could show that they had no choice, that neither they nor gay culture in general played any role in shaping their desires. Some conservatives, meanwhile, trivialize gay experience as "lifestyle," as though that warrants interfering with it. Both sides seem to agree on an insane assumption: that only immutable and genetic sexualities could be legitimate, that if being gay could be shown to be learned, chosen, or partly chosen, then it could be reasonably forbidden.

The biological, cultural, and individual factors in sexuality seem to be far too tightly woven for either side's reductive hopes. One of the genetic studies inadvertently illustrated this point. The study tracked the sexual preferences of identical twins reared apart, hoping to see whether genetic and individual factors could be distinguished. The researchers found a very striking case of male twins, separated from early childhood, both of whom shared the same sexual preference: masturbating over photos of construction workers. I don't imagine

anyone is ready to argue that there is a gene for the sexual orientation of masturbator-over-photos-of-construction-workers.
Whatever the genetic determinant might be, it isn't that. Nor
does it seem that the desire was simply chosen, as though we
could ever just choose any of our desires. Undeniably, many of
its components are features of cultural history, like the
medium of photography or the idea of "construction worker."
How could one begin to sort the "immutable" traits of such a
sexuality from the mutable ones? More important, why would
one need to do so? Is it only genetically determined desire that
deserves respect and legal protection? Could sexual autonomy
be limited to choices or desires that have been with us for all
time? On some accounts that would pretty much limit things
to men raping women, since little else can be shown to be natural and transhistorical.

The best historians of sexuality argue that almost everything about sex, including the idea of sexuality itself, depends
on historical conditions, though perhaps at deep levels of
consciousness that change slowly. "Heterosexual" and "homosexual" might be more similar to "masturbator-over-photos-
of-construction-workers" than most people think. As ways of
classifying people's sex, these apparently neutral terms are of
relatively recent vintage, and only make sense against a certain cultural background. So however much they might involve genetic or biological factors, they also involve changes
in consciousness and culture. The idea drives the moralists
crazy, but it shouldn't: any sexual ethics ought to allow for
change.

New fields of sexual autonomy come about through new
technologies: soap, razors, the pill, condoms, diaphragms,
Viagra, lubricants, implants, steroids, videotape, vibrators,
nipple clamps, violet wands, hormones, sex assignment surg-
eries, and others we can't yet predict. Some anatomical possi-

bilities that were always there, such as anal pleasure and female ejaculation, are learned by many only when the knowledge begins to circulate openly and publicly. The psychic dimensions of sex change as people develop new repertoires of fantasy and new social relations, like "white" or "construction worker," not to mention new styles of gender and shifting balances of power between men and women. Through long processes of change, some desires too stigmatized to be thought about gradually gain legitimacy, such as the desire for a homosexual lover. Others lose. Even desires now thought to be natural and normative, such as equal romantic love, only came into being relatively late in human history; they depend just as much on politics and cultural change as do the stigmatized ones.

Sex, in short, changes. As it does, the need for sexual autonomy changes. Some of the most familiar models of sexual liberation have not been very good at recognizing this. Freud, in *Civilization and Its Discontents,* speculated that the progress of civilization entailed ever higher levels of repression; for many of the leaders of the sexual liberation and gay liberation movements in the 1960s and '70s, the consequence seemed to be that freedom lay in reversing that trend, recovering kinds of sexual freedom that they associated with simpler times, or reclaiming the kind of polymorphously perverse sexuality that Freud associated with children. I do not dismiss this kind of thinking, since it led to many powerful analyses, and many liberation theorists, such as Herbert Marcuse, remain underappreciated. I am suggesting something different. Sex does not need to be primordial in order to be legitimate. Civilization doesn't just repress our original sexuality; it makes new kinds of sexuality. And new sexualities, including learned ones, might have as much validity as ancient ones, if not more.

What would it take to make sexual autonomy possible? The answer is not simply to roll back repression, loosen all constraints, purge ourselves from all civilized shame, return to an earlier state of development, run wild through the streets. (Anyone who wants to run wild down my street has my blessing.) Sexual autonomy has grown, not just by regressing to infantile pleasure (however important that might be), but by making room for new freedoms, new experiences, new pleasures, new identities, new bodies—even if many of us turn out to live in the old ones without complaining. Variation in this way is a precondition of autonomy—as much as it is also the outcome of autonomy. Pleasures once imaginable only with disgust, if at all, become the material out of which individuals and groups elaborate themselves.

Inequalities of shame act as a drag on this process. They inhibit variation and restrict knowledge about the variations that do exist. Moralities that insist on the permanence of sexual norms have an especially stunting effect on people who lack resources of knowledge or of experiment. As Wharton's story illustrates, there is a fine line between coercion through shame and constraint through ignorance. The more people are isolated or privatized, the more vulnerable they are to the unequal effects of shame. Conditions that prevent variation, or prevent the knowledge of such possibilities from circulating, undermine sexual autonomy. And the moralists work very hard to make sure that this happens.

The United States Supreme Court went so far in this effort as to exempt sexual materials from First Amendment protections. In *Roth v. the United States* (1957), it allowed states and the federal government to restrict anything defined as "obscene"—a word designed to shame dissenters into silence. The Court later defined obscenity as anything having "prurient" interest in sex and "offensive" by community standards.

Since community standards set the definition of obscene, the law in this area—unlike the rest of First Amendment law—allows the majority to impose its will without Constitutional check. Defenders of the law say that it imposes discretion and restraint on everyone. In fact it enlists the government in the politics of shame, making sure that nothing challenging to the tastes of the majority will be allowed to circulate.

The legal and political systems routinely produce shame simply in the pompous and corny way they force people to talk. Like many other states, for example, the state of Virginia has a law, enacted in 1950, that makes it a crime for any persons "to lewdly and lasciviously associate and cohabit together." This just means that sex outside of marriage, or merely living together, is illegal. The law is seldom enforced, and most people regard it as harmless anachronism. But it has real effects: people are denied child custody because it makes them criminal; gay men and lesbians have been fired from their jobs in some states on the same grounds; and defendants on other charges are often given tougher sentences by means of such statutes. (Sodomy laws are especially popular with prosecutors for this purpose.) Archaic legal language also has an effect simply by staying on the books and helping to create the air of unreality in which medieval moral judgments are given authority. Massachusetts law still refers to the "abominable and detestable crime against nature." Florida criminalizes "any unnatural and lascivious act." In the Wonderland of America's legal codes, the sex laws are like a version of Lewis Carroll's "Jabberwocky," with a vengeance: "Tis brillig, and the slithy toves did lewdly and lasciviously gyre and gimble in the wabe. All prurient were the borogoves, and the mome raths did fornicate." When the law talks this way, ordinary sexual knowledge goes on vacation, and the moralist's battle is more than half won.

Political debates have their own way of creating freakish weather conditions in which things that would have been too banal for Oprah suddenly attract lightning blasts from the heavens. In November of 1997, the State University of New York at New Paltz sponsored a conference titled "Revolting Behavior: The Challenges of Women's Sexual Freedom." Among the twenty-one panels were a workshop on female sexuality and a discussion of S/M. Sensing an opportunity to acquire political capital through shame, conservatives went into motion. Candace de Russy, a Republican appointee to the SUNY board of trustees, seemed to have attended the conference in order to denounce it, calling for the dismissal of New Paltz president Roger Bowen as soon as the conference ended. Roger Kimball wrote an essay for the *Wall Street Journal* calling the conference "a syllabus for sickos." Governor George Pataki, falling into line, denounced the conference and threatened to withhold state funding. SUNY chancellor John Ryan, calling the workshops "offensive," reprimanded Bowen for allowing them. None of this was really about improving education. It was a way to tap the vast power of sexual shame, disgust, and moralism for partisan ends. It failed in its stated goal of removing Bowen, but it succeeded in its real goal of mobilizing public scandal against sexual dissent. The chilling effect extended to my own school, Rutgers, where a feminist administrator nixed a graduate-student conference on women's sexuality for fear of replaying the controversy.

Unfortunately, the defenders of the conference fell back on weak arguments. Bowen justified it in the name of academic freedom and free speech, a line echoed by a *New York Times* editorial. Bowen argued that speech, "no matter how odious," cannot be restricted. He did not challenge the judgment that a workshop on sexuality is odious, like denying the

Holocaust. In fact, he went out of his way to say that he "personally found several of their planned panel topics offensive." He also did not respond to de Russy's substantive charge that the conference "had absolutely nothing to do with the college's undergraduate mission."

It isn't hard to understand Bowen's response. He had been put on the defensive by the conservative media machinery. Nothing in the education of college presidents prepares them to deal with the politics of sexual shame. It is hard to refute the sense that the subject is scandalous, since for so many people the demand for more shame simply feels like morality. Candace de Russy has a way of intoning the word "lesbianism" on camera with so much high-minded scorn that many people simply forget that the word might actually bring a lot of pleasure to others, or that others' pleasure costs them nothing, even if they do not share in it. And anyone who really believes in the university ideal of open discussion is likely to be unprepared for the silencing effect of sexual shame, especially when the media have jumped into the picture, amplifying ordinary shame into public scandal. The ideal of free speech probably seemed like the best defense he could imagine. It was a dodge.

A stronger and more honest response would have defended in substance the conference's goal of circulating knowledge and reflection about sexuality. Bowen might have pointed out, for example, that the study of sex need not be, as Roger Kimball claimed, "profoundly dehumanizing," a way of looking "at the sex organs as essentially a complicated piece of plumbing." Of course, complicated plumbing would be a perfectly legitimate thing to study, and the conservatives never complain about engineering conferences. Nor do they complain about biology seminars, which are much more likely to treat sex organs as plumbing than any panel of lesbians is likely to do. So why the fuss? And why "dehumaniz-ing"? From Plato's *Symposium* to contemporary queer theory, the study of sex has generally involved such fundamental questions as the relation of ethics to pleasure, the nature of consent, and the definition of freedom. What could be better questions for humanists to ask? If Kimball associates sexual knowledge with dehumanization, then that association in it-self might be important to study. If we were not sexual, would we be more human, or less? Why would ignorance be better? Who is dehumanizing whom? Minority sexualities often raise such questions in especially powerful ways.

Bowen might also have pointed out that the study of sex-uality, if it were asking such questions, could hardly avoid the shame and offensiveness that so many associate with the sub-ject. In fact, the conservative clamor about the conference could be taken as evidence of the way shame and oppro-brium can be much more than just natural responses of in-stinctual revulsion, and much more than a desire for privacy. They are political resources that some people use to silence or isolate others. As long as this is true, or even might be true, then talk about stigmatized sex is much more than indulgent shamelessness, or lack of respect for privacy. It is a necessary means to identify the political element of shame, to see how disgust and embarrassment are used by some to restrict the sexual autonomy of others. Circulating knowledge about sex, especially knowledge not already pleasing to "community standards," is a way to make that autonomy available in a less distorted way.

As sexual culture changes, it creates new needs for resist-ing shame. Ever since the idea of autonomy was first coupled with sex during the Enlightenment, one wave of unexpected resistance has followed another, from the women's movement to psychoanalysis to the lesbian and gay movement. Each has had to resist not just violence but the more normal kinds of sexual unfreedom: moralism, law, stigma, shame, and isolation. All of these constraints on people's autonomy might be in play anytime human beings seek to dominate one another. But in the realm of sex, more than in any other area of human life, shame rules.

SEXUAL McCARTHYISM AND THE POLITICS OF MORAL PANIC

If anyone doubts the power of sexual shame, one has to look no further for evidence than the Clinton impeachment. Of course, the issues in the Lewinsky affair were not likely to be confused with, say, the politics of lesbians and gay men. Bill Clinton, after all, was pilloried for the most stereotypically straight male sex, the kind of tacky, shameless, cigar-chomping erotics of power that is celebrated from the locker room to the boardroom. Yet to anyone who has experience in the politics of sexual stigma, and especially to gay men and lesbians, the crisis offered familiar ironies. Until Monicathon, it was always difficult to convince anyone in the public policy arena of the intensity of passions around sex, or of the destructive power of sexual stigma. Then Kenneth Starr's decision to focus on sex took the political system by surprise, leading to near meltdown.

There was nothing new about the stigmas he set in motion. They were the ordinary embarrassments of sex, amplified by the publicity of national politics and mass media. In this sex-phobic and sex-obsessed culture, sex has long been seen as intrinsically demeaning. For anyone to call attention to Bill Clinton's sex life—and above all, for a prosecutor to do so—was, inevitably, to humiliate him, far beyond anything that might be explained as merely moral or aesthetic disapproval of his sexual choices. This potent effect of indignity must have felt, for many gay men and lesbians, all too familiar.

So did the irrationality of the political system, suddenly driven home to everyone who had to watch the government self-destruct over thongs and semen stains. Postures of piety that would sound ridiculous in any other context seem to be the norm in the national media and official politics. Policy publics seem to have no way of recognizing sex as ordinary or as diverse. It is scandal or nothing. Not so in other contexts, of course. People know more about the messiness and variety of sex than they allow themselves to admit in public. This knowledge tends to remain inarticulate and often contradicts moral judgments to which people otherwise remain loyal. During the Clinton impeachment the knowledge of sex expressed itself as disgust with the politics of righteousness. The usual gap between official scandal and everyday sexual frankness widened, becoming a schizophrenic crisis that even the media managers of the corporate state could no longer control. The District of Columbia seemed to have gone drifting into a virtual world, beaming down broadcasts to a nation that no longer cared—at least in the way that it was told to care. The popular failure to be scandalized sent William Bennett into a hand-wringing, finger-wagging frenzy over "the death of outrage." This failure might not have expressed the amoral cynicism of the nation, as Bennett and other moralists thought; it might have expressed a realism about sex, and a recognition of the way shame works as a means to power. Suddenly everyone in politics looked phony, corny, and hypocritical. By seeing things this way, people were not demonstrating a lack of sexual ethics. They were, on the contrary, demonstrating an ethical insight into the politics of sexual shame.

Writing in the middle of the impeachment crisis, Alan Dershowitz called it "sexual McCarthyism." This was robust rhetoric, to be sure, and the antithesis of Bennett's "death of outrage." But it had an undeniably valid point: that the alignment of prudery, prosecution, and publicity was creating a moral panic that even the policy and media elites could no longer control. Some prosecutors gamely pretended that the sexual scandal was merely the occasion of a legal inquiry. Whatever the validity of the perjury and obstruction charges, that claim was disingenuous. Sexual shame is such that exposing it taints a person, no matter how moral or immoral the sex might otherwise be. The publicity given to sex was itself punitive. How could Clinton or Lewinsky challenge that humiliation? They didn't even try. To gay men and lesbians, this, too, might seem familiar.

Dershowitz thought the analogy between Clinton's experience and that of lesbians and gay men was more than a vague resemblance. Starr's prosecution followed directly in the footsteps of McCarthy's. McCarthyism the first time around, he claimed, took the form of queer hunting because that was the popular prejudice back then. (He seems to think this is no longer true.) Nowadays, the story goes, McCarthyism still targets sex, but it has moved on to presidential indiscretions. This story allows Dershowitz to score an important polemical point, but it blurs some important differences. The shame that Starr used to amplify his legal charges was not, after all, a way of stigmatizing identity. It would be hard to organize a movement (the Philandering Presidents' Liberation Front?) to fight against it. And the lesbian and gay organizations did not see this as their fight, for obvious reasons. Moreover, to tell the story the way Dershowitz tells it is to suggest that homophobia as a political force is a thing of the past, the form that an earlier moral panic happened to take, an aberration of the times.

At the same time, Dershowitz's narrative strikes a chord. It is true that modern history is littered with moral panics about sex, even more than he notes. Puritans under Elizabeth I thought that England was a new Sodom and that divine retribution was at hand, largely on account of sex. Many fled the English Sodom for America, where they worried about a New English Sodom and wrote legal codes explicitly modeled on Leviticus and Deuteronomy, including capital punishment for adultery. Panics about the sexual morality of cities, theaters, and courts were common from the Restoration of Charles II to the French Revolution, which was brought to a crisis in large part by a pornographic panic about Marie Antoinette's sex life. (The Clinton affair involved uncanny echoes of this episode.) The early nineteenth century saw a wave of antionanism campaigns and prostitution scares in America. From midcentury onward, miscegenation anxieties roiled whites into lynch mobs. The infamous Comstock law of 1873 criminalized obscenity and mandated censorship in the name of reform. White slave hysteria flowered at the turn of the century, and the twentieth century saw recurrent fits of queer hunting, especially in the American military. The Nazis built a program for sexual purification that fueled anti-Semitism and homophobia alike. In each case, and many others like them, sex deviance was blamed for dangers to the body politic. In each case, sexual coercion and violence were justified in the name of national health. McCarthy, in short, was the least of it.

Although moral panics tend to fall on a wide range of sexualities and sexual cultures, and not just on philandering presidents or homosexuals, I'm sure that to many gay men and lesbians the politics of sexual shame in the Clinton crisis made it seem as though one of the most familiar tales in their long history were suddenly being encountered by the rest of the nation for the first time. Clinton, certainly, was not the first to discover how hard it is in this culture to assert any dignity when you stand exposed as a sexual being. The Clinton impeachment may have been an extraordinary crisis, but perhaps less extraordinary than we would surmise from the chorus of commentators whose expressions of baffled astonishment radiated nightly from screen to shining screen.

Anglo-American culture has always been more prone to embarrassment about sex than most other cultures. Even to a casual observer, American culture presents a paradox. Of all nations, it is the most obsessed with sex, and of all nations it is the most easily scandalized. The United States is the land of sexual shame. This is often described as a Puritan streak in the culture. But after the Clinton presidency it would be hard to claim that America's weird mix of prurience and shame was simply a relic of ancient prejudice, doomed to wither in the course of history. Conflicts over sex in public are growing more common, not less. And nothing marks the obsessiveness of sex in this culture as much as the omnipresence of therapy, which is supposed to have eliminated old phobias. Everyone knows, supposedly, about the liberating effect of sexual candor. "Puritanical" is, with us, a bad word. Sexual taboos are a thing of the past, like girdles, or vacuum tubes, or Brylcreem. And yet people still fear and despise those whom they identify with sex. How can we explain this paradox?

Theodor Adorno, the great German philosopher who spent many years in America after fleeing Nazi Germany, was able to say as early as 1962 that attempts to reform the regulation of sex had "something venerably suffragette-like about them." But, he went on, people fool themselves about progress. Sexual taboos have not fallen away at all. "Whereas sexuality has been integrated, that which cannot be integrated, the actual spiciness of sex, continues to be detested by society." In fact, Adorno thought that this was true not despite the new premium on sexual expression, but because of it. In the American talk about a *healthy sex life* (and Adorno, writing in German, used the English phrase, which doubtless amused him), he saw the purest form of "a desexualization of sexuality itself." "Sexuality is disarmed as *sex*," he wrote, "as though it were a kind of sport, and whatever is different about it still causes allergic reactions."

Adorno showed his usual prescience in these comments. In 1962, of course, the gay rights movement was still small, without a well-developed theory of itself, without much public profile, and without an established social world. But Adorno embraced its cause. He saw that queers, like prostitutes, were going to bear the burden of the new paradox, as a culture that increasingly built itself around an entertainment industry of sex also found it increasingly necessary to insist that sex be hygienic and uplifting, that however "wild" it had to be to funnel optimism into the pseudo-individuality of consumer culture, it also had to be, at all times, healthy and normal.

It can seem at times that Americans think and talk about nothing but sex. Surely, many people say, after the Clinton trial we need less talk about sex rather than more, a sharper moral judgment rather than more skepticism. To them, the crisis represented the excess of sexual liberty, not the excess of sexual moralism. They think the end of the impeachment ordeal should mark the beginning of a new reserve, a revived sense of privacy and responsibility. This response can seem reasonable enough, partly because of the false sense of liberation that Adorno identified in consumer culture. Given the celebration of sport sex as a way of selling commodities, or distracting people from the banality of their mediatized and administered lives, it may be hard for many people to recognize any kind of variant sex as having ethical value. Then, too, coverage of the impeachment affair reeked of both fascinated pleasure and moralistic aversion—the combination that created the sense of scandal in the first place. Either way, the obsessiveness of our public media with sex does indeed feel salacious, fraudulent, and demeaning.

Yet moralism can hardly offer an adequate response. It only intensifies the oscillation of aversion and fascination that created the scandal. The obsession with sex in the great Monicathon of 1998 felt demeaning because it was never real recognition or acknowledgment; it never was really freed from the assumption that sex itself is demeaning, or "dehumanizing," as Roger Kimball put it. The fascinated inquisitiveness of national culture was driven not by a celebration of sexual pleasure and autonomy, but by erotophobia. The Clinton impeachment should show us, if nothing else, that erotophobia can take many forms besides silence, censorship, and repression. It can coexist with and even feed on commercialized titillation, desperate fascination, therapeutic celebration, and punitive prurience. So although sex is public in this mass-mediatized culture to a degree that is probably without parallel in world history, it is also true that anyone who is associated with actual sex can be spectacularly demonized.

This goes for anyone—straight, gay, or presidential. But some people are more exposed in their sexuality than others. Straight people can see a certain version of their straightness reflected back everywhere, from toothpaste ads to epic poems, and although they often rebel against the resulting banality of their sexual lives, they also profit from the way they seem no more sexually noticeable than anyone else. The ones who pay are the ones who stand out in some way. They become a lightning rod not only for the hatred of difference, of the abnormal, but also for the more general loathing for sex.

It is their sex, especially, that seems dehumanizing. What shocked many people about the Clinton scandal was the way he became a target for the kind of punitive attention usually reserved for sluts, queers, and trannies. Normally, straight male power sex is covered by a kind of tacit immunity agreement. Starr revoked it.

Dershowitz, in short, identified a much bigger problem than he realized when he spoke of sexual McCarthyism. Conflicts over sex have been fundamental to modern culture for at least as long as people have been speaking of democracy and autonomy. And although modern culture has learned to use public talk about sex as a stimulant to art and commerce alike, in the process some kinds of sexual shame have only intensified and become more political.

HIERARCHIES OF SHAME

What can we learn here about the politics of sexual shame? What exactly are the connections among the garden-variety embarrassments of sex, the spectacular crises of sexual McCarthyism, and the stigmatized identities of the gay movement? This question requires more thoughtful consideration than the blanket label "sexual McCarthyism" might suggest. But the connections, however complex, are real. Failing to recognize that there is a politics of sexual shame, I believe, leads to mistakes in each context: it confuses individuals, cowing them out of their sexual dignity; it leaves national politics pious and disingenuous about sex; and it reduces the gay movement to a desexualized identity politics.

In later chapters, we will see how the politics of shame distorts everything, from marriage law to public health policy, censorship, and even urban zoning. I also argue that the official gay movement—by which I mean its major national organizations, its national media, its most visible spokespersons—has lost sight of that politics, becoming more and more enthralled by respectability. Instead of broadening its campaign against sexual stigma beyond sexual orientation, as I think it should, it has increasingly narrowed its scope to those issues of sexual orientation that have least to do with sex. Repudiating its best histories of insight and activism, it has turned into an instrument for normalizing gay men and lesbians.

The mistake, in each of these cases, is a fundamental failure to understand the politics of sexual shame. In an influential 1984 essay called "Thinking Sex," Gayle Rubin suggested that the whole gamut of conflicts over sex—of the kind that crop up in every context, from office gossip and school board disputes to the highest levels of national and international policy—demonstrates a common dynamic. Sex has a politics of its own. Hierarchies of sex sometimes serve no real purpose except to prevent sexual variance. They create victimless crimes, imaginary threats, and moralities of cruelty. Rubin notes: "The criminalization of innocuous behaviors such as homosexuality, prostitution, obscenity, or recreational drug use is rationalized by portraying them as menaces to health and safety, women and children, national security, the family, or civilization itself." These rationalizations obscure the intent to shut down sexual variance.

Reviewing a wide range of sexual stigmas and regulations, Rubin contended that people sort good sex from bad by a series of hierarchies:

Good, Normal, Natural	Bad, Abnormal, Unnatural
Heterosexual	Homosexual
Married	Unmarried
Monogamous	Promiscuous

Procreative	Nonprocreative
Noncommercial	Commercial
In pairs	Alone or in groups
In a relationship	Casual
Same generation	Cross-generational
In private	In public
No pornography	Pornography
Bodies only	With manufactured objects
Vanilla	Sadomasochistic

These distinctions between good sex and bad do not nec-essarily come as whole packages; most people tend to mix traits from each column. The main thing the different distinc-tions have in common is the simple fact that each is a hierar-chy, and if you are on the wrong side of the hierarchy you will be stigmatized in a way that could entail real damage.

Bill Clinton got on the wrong side of several of these: he had sex outside marriage, did so promiscuously, and in pub-lic (the Oval Office!). Actually, Clinton and Lewinsky were lucky; if that blow job had taken place just across the Po-tomac River in Virginia, it would have been a felony, and even in the District of Columbia it was illegal until 1992. But the scandal had less to do with legal technicalities than with the taboos behind the law. And although there were doubtless many other grounds for thinking him unethical—his betrayal of private trust, his self-satisfied enjoyment of power—there can be no doubt that the sense of scandal came from the com-mon categories of deviance. When Republicans blew so hard in trumpeting their moral outrage, they were not moved by their concern for Hillary. They did not express a nuanced sense of Clinton's private ethical relation to Monica. They were moved by a more abstract sense of violated propriety, a crime not against any individual, but against the imaginary rules of sex. So Clinton might at least theoretically see himself as having something in common with people in all the other categories on the "wrong" side of the list. (I doubt that he has yet drawn this conclusion.)

Rubin would say that his transgressions do not necessarily mean that he scores worse on the sexual dignity scale than, say, someone whose only deviation was to be a transvestite. That is because these distinctions tend to be ranked in an ever-shifting continuum of more or less serious deviation, with a constant battle over "where to draw the line." As Rubin points out, some kinds of deviation have become more re- spectable over time. Others remain beyond the pale for all but the most radical or the most libertarian. Thus people who stray into the wrong category on one score or another may well reject with disdain any suggestion that they belong in al- liance with the perverts who stand below them on the scale of disgust. The people who drift into the right-hand column do not make common cause. If they did, the left-hand column wouldn't stand a chance of survival. Those who inhabit only the left-hand column are probably a tiny minority. And yet their scheme of value dominates.

One reason why people do not unite against shame is that there are some real differences among them. Here perhaps we should make an elementary distinction between stigma of the kind that gay people endure and shame of the kind that dogs Clinton. Rubin presents these as a continuum, but they differ in kind rather than degree, and the difference will turn out to be crucial to all of the examples studied in this book.

Stigma, like its etymological kin *stigmata,* refers to a mark on the body, like a brand or a tattoo or a severed ear, identify- ing a person permanently with his or her disgrace. Among the Greeks, it may have been punishment for a deed such as treason or running away from a master. It marked the person, not the deed, as tainted. This is what the modern metaphor of stigma singles out. It is a kind of "spoiled identity," as Erving Goffman calls it in his classic study. Ordinary shame, by contrast, passes. One might do a perverse thing and bring scorn or loathing on oneself, only to sober up and make excuses, move to a new town and start over, stay and outlive the memory, or redeem oneself by fine deeds. This kind of shame affects one's biographical identity. The shame of a true pervert—stigma—is less delible; it is a social identity that befalls one like fate. Like the related stigmas of racial identity or disabilities, it may have nothing to do with acts one has committed. It attaches not to doing, but to being; not to conduct, but to status.

Some of the dilemmas of the gay movement become clearer when we remember that it has had to combat both shame and stigma, and that they are often confused in practice. Sexual deviance once was more a matter of shame than of stigma. Sodomy was a sin like fornication, not the sign of an identity. Anyone could do it. In the modern world that shame has deepened into stigma. It affects certain people, regardless of what they do. As moralists began concentrating not simply on deeds but on kinds of persons, mere sex became sexuality. The act of sodomy came to be only one sign of homosexual identity among many. It became possible to suffer stigma as a homosexual quite apart from any sexual acts. Shame about sexual acts and the stigma on homosexual identity can be utterly distinct in some cases. But each has a tendency to blur into the other.

At first the distinction was the invention of medical experts, and worked only to the detriment of gay people. It was a way of saying that homosexuals were pathological in their very being, whether they ever committed an immoral act or not, simply by the nature of their desires. This pseudo-medical thinking raised perversion to a social identity. It fastened loathing and discrimination onto people in a way that had only a theoretical relation to any sex they might or might not have. Later, the same distinction became crucial to the gay resistance. The concept of perversion, as distinct from perverse acts, led to the concept of sexual identity (or its close kin, sexual orientation). Each distinguishes between identity and sex, between the person and the act, status and conduct. The doctors had inadvertently made it possible for their former patients to claim that being gay is not necessarily about sex. Homosexuals could argue that any judgment about their worth as persons, irrespective of their actions, was irrational prejudice. In so doing, they could challenge the stigma of identity, without in the least challenging the shame of sexual acts. To this day, a similar logic governs much of gay politics. That is why lawyers who challenge military antigay policy or discrimination by the Boy Scouts usually take pains to find test cases in which the victim is a model victim because he or she has never done anything wrong—that is, had sex.

When Clinton set out to reform the military antigay policy after his election in 1992, he made a point of saying that the military should be allowed to punish people for their acts, but not for their identities; the focus should be on "conduct, not status." He was invoking the most central premise of lesbian and gay politics as a politics of identity: that sexual orientation is fundamental to one's personality and is not mere sexual behavior. In making this argument, he was appealing to the same kind of distinction between doing and being that emerged a century before, when it first became common to think of some people as homosexual persons, whatever their sexual acts in fact were.

But this distinction proved difficult to observe. For one thing, the Supreme Court had blurred it in *Bowers v. Hard-*

wick. Although the Georgia sodomy statute that was the subject of that case applied to oral and anal sex for heterosexual partners as well as homosexual ones, the Court decided to regard the issue only as one of "homosexual sodomy" and the rights of homosexuals. The act—a kind of sex that gay or straight or bi or other people could equally perform—became an identity. In a dizzying series of logical moves, the Court ruled that Georgia could ban the sexual practice because of its connection to a despised identity, even though the law banned the practice for everybody. At the same time, the Court held that the identity could be (and in subsequent lower court decisions has been) regarded as fairly subject to discrimination because the sex, which "defines the class," was criminal. Gotcha: the sex has no privacy protection because homos are immoral; homos are immoral because they commit, or want to commit, criminal sex acts. As Janet Halley has shown, lawyers for the Department of Defense introduced the same circular equivocations to the revisions of military policy, and apparently Clinton never noticed that the one moral distinction he had laid down was now useless. The result is the notorious "Don't Ask, Don't Tell" policy, which punishes both act and identity, status and conduct—and under which military discharges for homosexuality have skyrocketed.

Just as the Supreme Court could utterly confuse status and conduct for legal purposes, so also lesbians and gay men often find in practice that the stigma on identity and the shame of sexual activity are hard to separate. That is not just because of the slipperiness of the Court's thinking. The prevailing ideas of sexual identity being what they are, when you come out as gay or lesbian the implication is that you have the same sexuality as all the others, including those compulsives crawling from orgasm to orgasm in the parks and gutters. The queer stigma covers us all, at least in some contexts.

As a consequence, people try to protect their identities by repudiating mere sex.

This confusion results from a basic paradox in the notion
of sexual identity. Identity, like stigma, tars us all with the
same brush, but it also allows us to distance ourselves from
any actual manifestation of queerness. We only share the
identity and its stigma, in fact, *because* identity has been distinguished from sexual acts and their shame. Pride or stigma
belongs to us as a class, a recognizable kind of person, regardless of our deeds as individuals. Thus there always seem
to be some gay people who are shocked, *shocked* to find that
others are having deviant sex. They will have you know that
their dignity is founded on being gay, which in their view has
nothing to do with sex. If others are having sex—or too much
sex or sex that is too deviant—then those people have every
reason to be ashamed. Of course only the playwright Larry
Kramer and a few other ranting moralists put it in these extreme terms, admittedly a caricature. And the distinction between stigma and shame, identity and act, is undeniable in
some contexts. But to have a politics of one without the other
is to doom oneself to incoherence and weakness. It is to challenge the stigma on identity, but only by reinforcing the
shame of sex. And unfortunately, this has been the choice not
only of individuals, but of much of the official gay movement.
In too many ways, it has chosen to articulate the politics of
identity rather than to become a broader movement targeting
the politics of sexual shame.

The core dilemma is ethical as well as political. Erving
Goffman captures its essence nicely, in a brilliant paragraph
about what he calls ambivalence:

> Whether closely allied with his own kind or not,
> the stigmatized individual may exhibit identity am-

bivalence when he obtains a close sight of his own kind behaving in a stereotyped way, flamboyantly or pitifully acting out the negative attributes imputed to them. The sight may repel him, since after all he supports the norms of the wider society, but his social and psychological identification with these offenders holds him to what repels him, transforming repulsion into shame, and then transforming ashamedness itself into something of which he is ashamed. In brief, he can neither embrace his group nor let it go.

On top of having ordinary sexual shame, and on top of having shame for being gay, the dignified homosexual also feels ashamed of every queer who flaunts his sex and his faggotry, making the dignified homosexual's stigma all the more justifiable in the eyes of straights. On top of that he feels shame about his own shame, the fatedness of which he is powerless to redress. What's a poor homosexual to do?

Pin it on the fuckers who deserve it: sex addicts, bodybuilders in Chelsea or West Hollywood, circuit boys, flaming queens, dildo dykes, people with HIV, anyone who magnetizes the stigma you can't shake. The irony is that in this culture, such a response will always pass as sexual ethics. Larry Kramer and other gay moralists have made careers out of it, specializing in what Goffman calls "in-group purification": "the efforts of stigmatized persons not only to 'normify' their own conduct but also to clean up the conduct of others in the group."

The dilemma of "identity ambivalence" has been an unmistakable force in the lesbian and gay movement from its inception. For individuals, it is a profound ethical challenge. This is true for people with any stigmatized identity, such as Jews or African Americans. But the dilemma is more tempting and more complicated for lesbians and gay men, or any other stigmatized sexuality. The distinction between stigma and shame makes it seem as though an easy way to resolve the ambivalence of belonging to a stigmatized group is to embrace the identity but disavow the act. As Kramer puts it, "The only response, the only way gays can assume our political responsibility and obtain our democratic due, is to fight for our rights *as gays*. To be taught about, to be studied, to be written about, not as cocks and cunts, but as *gays*." Kramer's distinction is not entirely mistaken. There is a real and consequential difference. But being lesbian or gay necessarily involves both stigma and shame. Kramer wants to fight one, but not the other. He can't even say it without spewing contempt for "cocks and cunts." He wants us to be more ashamed about sex, to see cocks and cunts as meriting even more scorn than we already have for them. And he wants us to direct this scorn toward other people who are more visibly identified with cocks and cunts than he wants to be. This is no way to escape the ambivalence of shame. Dignity on these terms is bound to remain inauthentic. (Perhaps that is why moralists of this variety seem permanently enraged.)

THE ETHICS OF QUEER LIFE

Defensiveness about sex and sexual variance is most common in public or official contexts. In many other circles, the idea of a gay man or lesbian posing as too mature or too respectable for mere sex is held to be ridiculous. For all the variety of queer culture—and all its limitations—it is possible to find, running through its development over the past century, and especially in its least organized and least "respectable" circles, an ethical vision much more at home with sex and with the indignities associated with sex. Nowhere, after all, are people more aware of the absurdity and tenacity of shame than in queer culture. That's why the official gay organizations' pious idea of a respectable, dignified gay community seems so out of keeping with the world those organizations claim to represent.

In the common gossip of friends catching up on girlfriends, in the magazines and videos that are sold and traded around and pored over, in the bars where hair of all kinds gets let down, in personal ads that declare tastes hitherto unknown to man, in scenes where some mad drag queen is likely to find the one thing most embarrassing to everyone and scream it at the top of her lungs, in Radical Faeries gatherings and S/M workshops—in these and other scenes of queer culture it may seem that life has been freed from any attempt at respectability or dignity. Everyone's a bottom, everyone's a slut, anyone who denies it is sure to meet justice at the hands of a bitter, shady queen, and if it's possible to be more exposed and abject then it's sure to be only a matter of time before someone gets there, probably on stage and with style. The fine gradations of nerviness that run through this culture measure out people's willingness to test the limits of shame. In these scenes people try to imagine living without the sacrifices that dignity by "community standards" commonly entails. Across town, where the black-tie fund-raiser is going on, that's where to find talk of dignity, if you have a taste for that sort of thing.

No wonder this sexual culture, which has often been underground and remains foreign to many gay men and lesbians, has seldom been regarded as a place to go for ethical insight into dignity, sex, and shame—neither by philosophers in general nor even by leaders of the gay movement. It seems to be an anarchic gutter zone more remarkable for the absence of ethics than for any tradition of insight. So, at least, it would be easy to think. I think this is a mistake. I am not the first to think so; Jean-Paul Sartre, for example, erected an elaborate edifice of moral thought on the basis of Jean Genet's queer writing in his *Saint Genet*—a book that the moralists would do well to revisit. But Sartre was concerned to illustrate problems of freedom and autonomy, and he left aside the public questions of sexual culture.

In those circles where queerness has been most cultivated, the ground rule is that one doesn't pretend to be *above* the indignity of sex. And although this usually isn't announced as an ethical vision, that's what it perversely is. In queer circles, you are likely to be teased and abused until you grasp the idea. Sex is understood to be as various as the people who have it. It is not required to be tidy, normal, uniform, or authorized by the government. This kind of culture is often denounced as relativist, self-indulgent, or merely libertine. In fact, it has its own norms, its own way of keeping people in line. I call its way of life an ethic not only because it is understood as a better kind of self-relation, but because it is the premise of the special kind of sociability that holds queer culture together. A relation to others, in these contexts, begins in an acknowledgment of all that is most abject and least reputable in oneself. Shame is bedrock. Queers can be abusive, insulting, and vile toward one another, but because abjection is understood to be the shared condition, they also know how to communicate through such camaraderie a moving and unexpected form of generosity. No one is beneath its reach, not because it prides itself on generosity, but because it prides itself on nothing. The rule is: Get over yourself. Put a wig on before you judge. And the corollary is that you stand to learn most from the people you think are beneath you. At its best, this ethic cuts against every form of hierarchy you could bring into the room. Queer scenes are the true *salons des refusés,* where the most heterogeneous people are brought into great intimacy by their common experience of being despised and rejected in a world of norms that they now recognize as false morality.

For this reason, paradoxically, the ethic of queer life is actually truer to the core of the modern notion of dignity than the usual use of the word is. Dignity has at least two radically different meanings in our culture. One is ancient, closely related to honor, and fundamentally an ethic of rank. It is historically a value of nobility. It requires soap. (Real estate doesn't hurt, either.) The other is modern and democratic. Dignity in the latter sense is not pomp and distinction; it is inherent in the human. You can't, in a way, not have it. At worst, others can simply fail to recognize your dignity. These two notions of dignity have opposite implications for sex. The most common judgments about sex assign dignity to some kinds (married, heterosexual, private, loving), as long as they are out of sight, while all other kinds of sex are no more dignified than defecating in public, and possibly less so. That kind of dignity we might as well call bourgeois propriety. In what I am calling queer culture, however, there is no truck with bourgeois propriety. If sex is a kind of indignity, then we're all in it together. And the paradoxical result is that only when this indignity of sex is spread around the room, leaving no one out, and in fact binding people together, that it begins to resemble the dignity of the human. In order to be consistent, we would have to talk about dignity in shame. That, I think, is a premise of queer culture, and one reason why people in it are willing to call themselves queer—a word that, as Eve Sedgwick notes, emblazons its connection to shame in a way that still roils the moralists. But I'm speaking now of sluts and drag queens and trannies and trolls and women who have seen a lot of life—not of the media spokesmen and respectable leaders of the gay community.

The lesbian and gay movement at its best has always been rooted in a queer ethic of dignity in shame. This is what Stonewall stands for. A political movement based in this kind of dignity, however, should extend far beyond questions of sex or sexual identity. The stigma that we call homophobia, after all, can descend on people for a lot of different reasons, and many of them are not exactly the same as being gay or homosexual. People whose gender identity differs from the norm are despised, often violently, whether they desire those of their own sex or not. Nelly boys and butch girls can be fag-bashed or taunted, and being heterosexual will not protect them very much. In the same contexts, homosexuals whose gender conforms more to the norm can often be silently accepted. And people whose gender identity and object choice both pass as normal can nonetheless find themselves despised as queer because of their sexual practice. Prostitutes are the most visible examples, as are people in leather culture. Even fairly conventional heterosexual married couples often find that they enjoy anal play, sex toys, sex in public places, sadomasochism, etcetera, and these practices expose them to shame, moralism, and even prosecution in some cases. (Sex toys remain illegal in Texas and Alabama; anal and oral sex in many more states.) It's even true that people of very unremarkable gender identity, object choice, *and* sexual practice might still passionately identify with and associate with queer people. Subjectively, they feel nothing of the normalcy that might be attributed to them.

Stigma is messy and often incoherent. The received wisdom, in straight culture, is that all of its different norms line up, that one is synonymous with the others. If you are born with male genitalia, the logic goes, you will behave in masculine ways, desire women, desire feminine women, desire them exclusively, have sex in what are thought to be normally active and insertive ways and within officially sanctioned contexts, think of yourself as heterosexual, identify with other heterosexuals, trust in the superiority of heterosexuality no matter how tolerant you might wish to be, and never change any part of this package from childhood to senescence. Heterosexuality is often a name for this entire package, even though attachment to the other sex is only one element. If you deviate at any point from this program, you do so at your own cost. And one of the things straight culture hates most is any sign that the different parts of the package might be recombined in an infinite number of ways. But experience shows that this is just what tends to happen. If heterosexuality requires the entire sequence, then it is very fragile. No wonder it needs so much terror to induce compliance.

There is no way of predicting how many people might in this way have a stake in a political movement against the effects of sexual stigma and shame. Queer culture tends to expand the possibilities. Strap-on dildos, for example, are no longer a lesbian-only item; they are increasingly used for role-reversal by opposite-sex couples. When activist Carol Queen produced a videotape called *Bend Over Boyfriend,* it became the fastest-selling video ever at San Francisco's principal sex-toy store, Good Vibrations. It will never be everyone's taste, but it might be anyone's.

The term "queer" is used in a deliberately capacious way in this book, as it is in much queer theory, in order to suggest how many ways people can find themselves at odds with straight culture. "Homophobia" is a misleading term for what they equally resist, because it suggests that the stigma and oppression directed against this entire range of people can be explained simply as a phobic reaction to same-sex love. In fact, sexual stigmas are more shifty than we think. Gay men and lesbians have been a principal target, but a political movement that defines its constituency solely as "gay men and lesbians" blinds itself both to the subtlety of the oppressive culture and to the breadth of the possible resistances. Already, the movement has been forced to add "bisexual" and, occasionally, "transgendered" to its self-description. These gestures are often rightly perceived, especially by bisexuals and transgendered people, as afterthoughts, half-hearted gestures at being politically correct.

Even at its most serious, this new, expanded list of "lesbian-gay-bisexual-transgendered" does not go far enough in naming what's at stake in queer politics. Like "gay and lesbian," it names identities that may or may not have anything to do with actual sex. But it is also true that sex can be stigmatized, or become a target for phobic reaction, in ways that are not focused on these kinds of identity. More typically, sex and identity can simply be confused with each other. So even an expanded catalog of identities can remain blind to the ways people suffer, often indiscriminately, from gender norms, object-orientation norms, norms of sexual practice, and norms of subjective identification. This sounds abstract, but in practice it is often instinctively understood in many contexts, from street scenes to drag performance clubs to some service organizations and AIDS groups. In these places, it is possible to have a concrete sense of being in the same boat with people who may not share your sexual tastes at all—people who have had to survive the penalties of dissent from the norms of straight culture, for reasons that may be as various as the people themselves.

The organized gay movement, as we will see in the following chapters, has in many ways lost that vision. The point of a movement is to bring about a time when the loathing for queer sex, or gender variance, will no longer distort people's lives. In the meantime, we (or some of us, acting in the name of homosexuals) try to clean ourselves up as legitimate players in politics and the media. As a movement we resort to a temporary pretense: "We're gay," we say, "but that has nothing to do with sex." And then, too often, this stopgap pretense is mistaken for the desired utopia. No more sex! Free at last!

These contradictions haunt us, both as individuals and as a movement. The movement in too many ways has chosen to become a politics of sexual identity, not sex. But it can never really escape its reliance on a sex public, nor the loathing that continues to be attached to any explicit or publicly recognized sex. Scandal hangs over our head even when we are in our Sunday finest—especially then. And although this tension is felt across the entire movement (in a way that is unique to queer politics), it also creates a tendency to sort people by greater or lesser degrees of privilege. A hierarchy emerges. Some people pay a higher price for the loathing of queer sexuality (or gender variance) than others. In the right social quarters, if you behave yourself, you can have a decent life as a normal homo—at least, up to a point. Those with the biggest fig leaves stand, always, at the top of the hierarchy. The only price they pay is the price of contradiction. They must claim that, though defined by sexuality, they are beyond it.

The American gay movement repeats within itself, in exaggerated form, the contradictions that Adorno already identified with America on the basis of his experience in California. And if conflicts over sex have become so much more prominent in the national culture, it is not surprising that similar stresses should appear in queer politics, which brings them to such a pitch of intensity. The sad truth is that the movement has never been able to resolve its sense that dignity and sex are incompatible. Some ways of relieving this tension are worse than others, and, as we shall see in the next chapter, at the moment those are the ones that are winning.

CHAPTER TWO

WHAT'S WRONG WITH NORMAL?

"Normalcy is the evil side of homosexuality."
—*Jack Smith*

In 1998, at the height of the American Monicathon, a new gay magazine appeared. Called *Hero*, it had one purpose: to give gays and lesbians a magazine without sex. No sexy underwear ads, no personals, no ads for phone sex or adult web sites, no stories on sex, no ads for HIV medications. "We're not political, and we're not making a statement," the editor told one gay newspaper. Presumably he did not want the magazine confused with the moralistic rants of the playwright Larry Kramer, who for decades has been calling for a desexed gay movement. *Hero*'s editor explained to the *New York Blade*, a gay newspaper, that the idea for the magazine came when he published an article in a gay magazine. When the piece appeared, it was followed by a phone-sex ad. "All of a sudden," he reports, "I feel like I'm reading some kind of pornography. I ended up ripping it out and sending my mother the clip, but I thought, 'What am I doing?' I want to be able to show her a magazine."

This is a classic example of the problem of ambivalence that we saw in the last chapter. A gay man, feeling the embarrassment of stigma, feeling cut off from the heterosexual world (in the person of Mom), and feeling that this stigma is something he does not deserve by his actions, that his actions (writing an article) are in fact meritorious, finds in the behavior of others in his group the real cause of his own stigma. It seems like a perfectly logical conclusion to him: to gain respect, to erase the barrier of stigma that shames him before his mother, he must purify the group. And the way to do that, for a gay man, is to redeem gay identity by repudiating sex. Whether the editors intended it or not, then, the magazine is one small token of the politics of shame.

A new magazine is not in itself a noteworthy trend, and the founding of *Hero* may be significant only as the latest expression of this familiar ambivalence. But the editors are disingenuous in claiming not to be political. The magazine's masthead proclaims, "THE MAGAZINE FOR THE REST OF US." It augurs a new PG gay movement. Apparently, "the rest of us" (unlike the other kinds of us) want a gay movement you could take home to Mom. And the first thing that has to go is the sex. The personal drama of ambivalence has been translated into a story about the direction of the gay movement. But on behalf of whom? Who, in fact, are "the rest of us"? A faceless mass, defined only by negation? A silent majority of "normal" homosexuals?

Tensions over sex have marked the gay movement from the outset, as we have seen. Those tensions have taken a new and urgent form within the American gay movement. Some of this is merely a matter of spin, like the masthead of *Hero*. I think it is more than that; there are reasons why this spin has become especially powerful in the movement now, and the emergence of so many slick lifestyle magazines like *Hero* is one of those reasons. But that spin works only because it appeals to the ambivalence that gay men and lesbians have over stigma and shame.

What's more, it works because identity ambivalence affects not just individuals, but political groups and magazines, the public interfaces of gay life. For them, the ambivalence of stigma is not just a psychic tension, but a structuring principle, a law of existence. Their role is to mediate between the world where lesbian and gay people gather and the dominant culture. Erving Goffman coined names for these two poles of tension: he referred to the "stigmaphile" space of the stigmatized among themselves, and the "stigmaphobe" world of the normals. The stigmaphile space is where we find a commonality with those who suffer from stigma, and in this alternative realm learn to value the very things the rest of the world despises—not just because the world despises them, but because the world's pseudo-morality is a phobic and inauthentic way of life. The stigmaphobe world is the dominant culture, where conformity is ensured through fear of stigma. Political organizations and public institutions like magazines find it necessary to speak in both directions, in ways that can be understood by both audiences at once. The conflicts and ambivalences inherent in this position can be resolved in different ways, creating a spectrum of political groups with greater loyalty to one side or the other. Those closest to the stigmaphile world will express the most radical political defiance. Those closest to the stigmaphobe world will express the most reluctance, the greatest desire for a conformity that yet can never finally be achieved.

In the case of gay groups, it might seem that we therefore have an inevitable tension, with sex radicals at one end and assimilationists at the other. People at both ends seem to see the tension in these terms: many at the stigmaphobe end accuse the sex radicals of embracing their victimhood, or creating "a cult of the outsider." Many at the stigmaphile end, meanwhile, accuse their opponents of "internalized homophobia." Because some such tension is structural to the politics of stigmatized groups, we might think that it will just never go away, and we should resign ourselves to it, rather than try to resolve these perpetual differences of perspective.

I am not so easily resigned. For one thing, the conflict here is far from being an equal tension. It is a hierarchy. Political groups that mediate between queers and normals find that power lies almost exclusively on the normal side. The more you are willing to articulate political issues in a way that plays to a normal audience, the more success you are likely to have. The more a political or cultural group defines itself in this way, of course, the more it is likely to be staffed and supported by individuals who have resolved their personal ambivalence in the same way. So although there is no direct or necessary link between one's ethical posture and one's access to power or wealth—there are very queer people who are wealthy, or who are active in upper political echelons, while there are people in grassroots groups who are quite susceptible to the bribes of shame—still, there is a tendency for wealth and power to accrue on the stigmaphobe side of the normals.

Thus the dialogue is unequal, distorted. The worst irony is that the stigmaphobe group will claim to represent the others. It will present itself as more general in scope and more respectable in tone. It will, in consequence, gain power. Yet given the dynamic of ambivalence, it is the group closest to respectability that is least likely to have made its peace with sexual shame. To the extent that the movement shifts from being a politics of stigma, rooted in a queer ethic, to being a caucus or service for homosexuals, the balance of power within the movement shifts toward these people; that is, the ones who have the most power anyway. This kind of shift in power has been unmistakable in the 1990s, but its roots lie deep in the movement's history.

THE GAY AND LESBIAN MOVEMENT AND THE AMBIVALENCE OF IDENTITY

The gay and lesbian movement is America's longest-running sex scandal. It might have been expected to end all sexual scandal once and for all, to declare an end to the days of shame, bringing sex out of the closet and into the daylight, letting all the gerbils scamper free. Its leaders, especially, might have become, by this late date, unembarrassable. But that hasn't happened. Many of the leaders and organizations of the gay and lesbian movement continue to be defensive about sex and sexual variance. As we will see, the aura of scandal has been heightened by many of the movement's spokespersons themselves, who have increasingly called for a "new maturity," beyond mere sex. These are upright and leaderly notes to strike on the podium, but the more one thinks this way the more actual sex will continue to be a source of discomfort. And when couched in a language of morality, that discomfort turns into the kind of sexual McCarthyism that has come to mark not only American national culture during the Monicathon but also the gay movement itself.

From the forming of the Mattachine Society in 1950 to the present, the indignity of sex has not ceased to hound the movement's leaders. The first real success of the Mattachine Society followed the arrest of one of its original members, Dale Jennings, for lewdness. Like pop star George Michaels in

1998, he was arrested in the bathroom of a public park. His 1953 article about the stigma he felt from the arrest shows that he remained deeply conflicted about it. The Mattachine Society at the time aspired to a strong vision of change, partly because its founders had their formative experience with the labor movement and the Communist Party, but also because they wanted to cultivate a distinct sense of a minority culture and its ethics. Successfully challenging the arrest as police entrapment, they used this success as a rallying point for new members. By 1953, though, distrust of left-wing politics and of cultural distinctness led to a revolt from within. The founders of the organization were forced out of the leadership. One lesbian among the new leaders declared that homosexuals would gain equality only by "integrating," by insisting on being "men and women whose homosexuality is irrelevant to our ideals, our principles, our hopes and aspirations."

This self-defeating language discloses the whole sad comedy from which the lesbian and gay movement has yet to emerge. Sex and sexuality are disavowed as "irrelevant" in an attempt to fight stigma. But the disavowal itself expresses the same stigma! It is not hard to understand the appeal of this language. It expresses the utopian notion that somewhere, one might not be defined by one's sexuality, that stigma might simply vanish from among the living. But since that utopia exists nowhere in *this* culture's near future, the idea reads as wishfulness, or even as self-contradiction. It is hard to claim that homosexuality is irrelevant as long as you feel the need to make the claim. If sexuality really were "irrelevant to our ideals, our principles, our hopes and aspirations," we wouldn't have much to say to one another. We certainly wouldn't have a movement. Organizations such as the Mattachine Society itself are nothing if not a framework of ideals, principles, hopes, etcetera, and sexuality is not just relevant to those organizations—it defines them. So if it really were possible to imagine no relevant connection between sex and respectable personhood, then one might as well go back to fucking in the bushes and have no politics at all.

In changing their creed, the new leaders of the Mattachine Society were being worse than merely wishful or contradictory. They implicitly confirmed the dominant assumption that homosexuality is itself unworthy. If sex is an indignity to be borne, then the less relevant it might be to anything, the better. Try imagining, by contrast, that heterosexuality might be irrelevant to the normative organization of the world. People are constantly encouraged to believe that heterosexual desire, dating, marriage, reproduction, childrearing, and home life are not only valuable to themselves, but the bedrock on which every other value in the world rests. Heterosexual desire and romance are thought to be the very core of humanity. It is the threshold of maturity that separates the men from the boys (though it is also projected onto all boys and girls). It is both nature and culture. It is the one thing celebrated in every film plot, every sitcom, every advertisement. It is the one thing to which every politician pays obeisance, couching every dispute over guns and butter as an effort to protect family, home, and children. What would a world look like in which all these links between sexuality and people's ideals were suddenly severed? Nonstandard sex has none of this normative richness, this built-in sense of connection to the meaningful life, the community of the human, the future of the world. It lacks this resonance with the values of public politics, mass entertainment, and mythic narrative. It matters to people primarily in one area of life: when it brings queers together. Gay political groups owe their very being to the fact that sex draws people together and that in doing so it suggests alternative possibilities of life. How ironic, then, that so often the first act of gay political groups is to repudiate sex.

The contradiction played well, evidently, to the rank and file of the Mattachine Society, especially since it came at the height of McCarthy's red-baiting and queer-hunting crusade. The new leaders called for a "pattern of behavior that is acceptable to society in general and compatible with [the] recognized institutions . . . of home, church, and state." To normal America—the America of home, church, and state—sex, or at least other people's sex, was by definition not ethical. The challenge, and the Mattachine Society tackled it bravely, was to build a movement of homosexuals without sex.

Even after fifty years of resistance, loathing for queer sex, like loathing for gender nonconformity, remains powerful enough to make the lesbian and gay movement recoil, throwing up its gloved hands in scandalized horror at the sex for which it stands. The movement has never been able to escape some basic questions: How is it possible, for example, to claim dignity for people defined in part by sex, and even by the most undignified and abject sex? Is the demand for dignity, propriety, and respectability hopelessly incompatible with the realities of sex? Is it entirely unreasonable that so many gay men and lesbians have seen the demand for respectability as a false ethics, choosing instead to explore in defiance all the taboos of abject need and shame? What kind of politics could be based in such a refusal to behave properly?

I take these to be serious and tough questions. Too often, though, the response to them in gay and lesbian politics has been defensive and apologetic. Gay people, it is said, are not really so bad. It's just a few extremists giving a bad name to ordinary decent folk. And of course it is true enough that many gay men and lesbians have had little to do with the ex-

tremes of queer sexual culture. They might be happily coupled veterinarians in a suburban tract home with nothing
more scandalous on their minds than wearing white linen after Labor Day. Well, bully for them. The problem comes
when it is said that this makes them more respectable, easier
to defend, the worthier pillars of the community, and the real
constituency of the movement—"the rest of us." Through
such a hierarchy of respectability, from the days of the Mattachine Society to the present, gay and lesbian politics has been
built on embarrassment. It has neglected the most searching
ethical challenges of the very queer culture it should be protecting.

This tendency to reproduce the hierarchy of shame, I believe, results from the structuring conditions of gay and lesbian politics, and not from the bad intentions of the people
who devote their lives to activism within the movement. By
national standards sex scandals remain extraordinary affairs.
For gays and lesbians, they are the norm. As soon as a movement was organized, embarrassment became a permanent
condition of its politics. On one side, the movement must appeal to its constituency—people who often have nothing in
common other than their search for a sexual world and the
shame and stigma that such a search entails. They turn to
movement politics in part to elaborate and glue together the
world in which they find and define one another, including
their sexual culture. On the other side, that movement attempts to win recognition for these sorry sluts and outcasts,
wringing a token of dignity from the very culture that produces and sustains so much shame and stigma in the first
place. Drawing the curtain over the sexual culture without
which it could not exist, it speaks whatever language of respectability it thinks will translate. The tension between these
two standards, internal and external, defines gay and lesbian

politics, saddling its spokespersons with difficult dilemmas. Can it be very surprising if those who are most concerned with winning respect might find themselves wishing that their peers in shame would be a little less queer, a little more decent?

For all these reasons, aversion to sex has been a constant problem in the half-century of organized gay and lesbian politics. Even after Stonewall, in the heyday of "gay liberation," the problem never quite went away. In 1981, for example, the National Organization of Lesbians and Gays (NOLAG) was no sooner founded than it foundered, in a bitter dispute over a "sexual freedom resolution" coauthored by Junel Bellwether and Susie Bright. Like most stigmatized groups, gays and lesbians were always tempted to believe that the way to overcome stigma was to win acceptance by the dominant culture, rather than to change the self-understanding of that culture. Alternatively some lesbians, like many other feminists, argued that sex was too deeply shaped by the dominant culture—that the sexualization of women was too much a part of their domination by men—for sex to be regarded with anything better than suspicion. A wave of antiporn and antisex feminism in the late 1970s led to a dramatic controversy over the 1982 conference on women's sexuality at Barnard College. In response, lesbians and other feminists fought the antiporn argument with searching analyses of pleasure and power in the so-called "sex wars" of 1980s feminism. Their work made possible a prosex and anticensorship lesbian feminism that is even now powering new and flourishing forms of lesbian sexual culture.

For gay men of the 1980s, however, AIDS gave new life to the ancient assumption that sex, and especially queer sex, had to be unethical—unhealthy, irresponsible, immature, and, in short, threatening to home, church, and state. For example, while bathhouses in other countries became valuable places for developing a culture of safer sex, in the United States they became the focus of a crackdown more convinced of its righteousness than ever. The Gay and Lesbian Alliance Against Defamation (GLAAD) had its genesis in the fight against this crackdown in 1985 (but don't expect such courage from GLAAD these days). The AIDS Coalition to Unleash Power—commonly known as ACT UP—which shortly followed, made the recognition and affirmation of queer sex central to its strategies of political resistance and HIV prevention. AIDS activism in its most powerful (and truly ethical) mode was formed by the need to confront the pseudo-ethics that consisted in a willingness to stigmatize those who had sex, to blame them for the virus that was killing them, to use their sex as an excuse to let them die, to prevent at all cost any further talk of sex even if it could be shown—as it was—that safer sex was the best and healthiest and most ethical solution to the crisis of prevention. AIDS activists learned quickly that effective prevention cannot be based on shame and a refusal to comprehend; it requires collective efforts at honest discussion, a realism about desire and a respect for pleasure. Yet the whistles and chants of AIDS activism had hardly begun to die down before the same old pseudo-ethics began to be heard in a different form—this time dressed up as a new maturity, the coming of age of the gay movement after AIDS, after AIDS activism, and after sex. Now, as the memory of direct action fades, that revisionist narrative can all too easily pass as common sense.

One reason why we have not learned more from this history is that queers do not have the institutions for common memory and generational transmission around which straight culture is built. Every new wave of queer youth picks up something from its predecessors but also invents itself from scratch. Many are convinced that they have nothing to learn from old dykes and clones and trolls, and no institutions—neither households nor schools nor churches nor political groups—ensure that this will happen. And since the most painfully instructed generation has been decimated by death, the queer culture of the present faces more than the usual shortfall in memory. Now younger queers are told all too often that a principled defense of nonnormative sex is just a relic of bygone "liberationism." This story is given out in bland confidence, since so many of the people who would have contradicted it have died.

Throughout this history, from the Mattachine Society to the present, runs a central conflict over the ethics of sexual shame. At each moment, the question boils down to this: dignity on whose terms? Increasingly, the answer is that to have dignity gay people must be seen as normal. It is widely believed (though just how widely would be difficult to say) that the gay movement has turned in this direction in the 1990s. Not assimilationist, exactly, but normalizing. And this shift in direction is widely believed to represent the interests of a silent majority of gay people—the rest of us.

WHY NORMAL?

In the issue of *The New Republic* that hit the streets just in time for the 1993 March on Washington, Andrew Sullivan—then the magazine's editor—wrote a manifesto that turns out to have been the most influential gay essay of the '90s. He called on gays to abandon "the notion of sexuality as cultural subversion," which, he said, "alienated the vast majority of gay people who not only accept the natural origin of their sexual orientation, but wish to be integrated into society as it is." For these people, "a 'queer' identity is precisely what they want to avoid," and a responsible gay politics should be about helping them avoid it. Most gay people, Sullivan went on to argue in his 1995 book, *Virtually Normal*, want to be seen as normal; and with some achievements in civil rights and the increasing visibility of gay people in the culture, they are almost there.

Sullivan's main argument here has had an extremely powerful influence, even on people who otherwise disagree with the often cantankerous and eccentric Sullivan. Nearly everyone, it seems, wants to be normal. And who can blame them, if the alternative is being abnormal, or deviant, or not being one of the rest of us? Put in those terms, there doesn't seem to be a choice at all. Especially not in America, where normal probably outranks all other social aspirations. What immortality was to the Greeks, what *virtù* was to Machiavelli's prince, what faith was to the martyrs, what honor was to the slave owners, what glamou,r is to drag queens, normalcy is to the contemporary American. Of course people want individuality as well, but they want their individuality to be the normal kind, and given the choice between the two they will take normal. But what exactly is normal?

Answers to this question tend to be statistical. One reason why you won't find many eloquent quotations about the desire to be normal in Shakespeare, or the Bible, or other common sources of moral wisdom, is that people didn't sweat much over being normal until the spread of statistics in the nineteenth century. Now they are surrounded by numbers that tell them what normal is: census figures, market demographics, opinion polls, social science studies, psychological surveys, clinical tests, sales figures, trends, the "mainstream," the current generation, the common man, the man on the street, the "heartland of America," etcetera. Under the conditions of mass culture, they are constantly bombarded by images of statistical populations and their norms, continually invited to make an implicit comparison between themselves and the mass of other bodies.

Since the publication of Alfred Kinsey's *Sexual Behavior in the Human Male* in 1948, they have also had a steady diet of statistics about sex. People have come to rely on these numbers in evaluating the validity of their own sex lives. As Mary Poovey notes, in a devastating essay about the sex study published as *Sex in America,* "According to the authors of *Sex in America,* normal Americans are driven by the desire to be normal—and to know that they, and especially their sexual behaviors, are already normal. . . . Further, the form that information must take to convince normal readers that they are normal is statistical—for, by the authors' own account, numbers metamorphose almost inevitably into the kind of evaluative thinking that makes people who belong to the statistical majority feel superior to those who do not."

Poovey's comment raises the interesting question of why anyone would *want* to be normal. If normal just means within a common statistical range, then there is no reason to be normal or not. By that standard, we might say that it is normal to have health problems, bad breath, and outstanding debt. One might feel reassured that one is not the only person to have these things, but the statistics only help with one's embarrassment; they say nothing about the desirability of the things themselves. It is *not* normal to be a genius, die a virgin, or be well endowed. That, again, tells us nothing about what one should want.

Moreover, to be fully normal is, strictly speaking, impossible. Everyone deviates from the norm in some way. Even if one belongs to the statistical majority in age group, race, height, weight, frequency of orgasm, gender of sexual partners, and annual income, then simply by virtue of this unlikely combination of normalcies one's profile would already depart from the norm. Then, too, the idea of normal is especially strange in the realm of sex. In one sense, nothing could be more normal than sex. Like eating, drinking, and breathing, it's everywhere. In another sense, though, sex can never be normal. It is disruptive and aberrant in its rhythms, in its somatic states, and in its psychic and cultural meaning.

More than anyone else, Alfred Kinsey was able to exploit the confusion at the heart of normal. One of his most dramatic points was that nonnormative sexual activities are, in fact, the statistical norm. Using his (admittedly unreliable) figures for things like extramarital sex and same-sex encounters, he calculated that 95 percent of the male population had committed some illicit sexual activities punishable by law. "Only a relatively small proportion of the males who are sent to penal institutions for sex have been involved in behavior which is materially different from the behavior of most of the males in the population. But it is the total 95 per cent of the male population for which the judge or board of public safety, or church, or civic group demands apprehension, arrest, and conviction, when they call for a clean-up of the sex offenders in a community." Kinsey almost certainly exaggerated these figures, if only inadvertently through his irregular sampling. Yet the cataclysmic cultural impact of his study depended less on any of his numbers than on his central point about the contradictory idea of the normal. The idea of normal sexuality, he argued, is too distorted by moralism to be an accurate picture of normal behavior, and if people really were willing to accept behavioral norms as normal, then their sexual morality would have to be radically different.

So why is it so important to people that they be normal? Is it normal to want to be normal? There can be no doubt that something odd is going on in the common use of the term.

When people want to be normal they might be partly under the influence of an association of the term that has become somewhat archaic in English, in which normal means certified, approved, as meeting a set of normative standards. This is why teachers' colleges are called normal schools. In French the association remains strong, and when one speaks of normalization, one refers to the whole process of training, testing, and authorizing people as full members of society. The deep sense of judgment and higher authority embedded in the idea of the normal may owe something to this sense of the term, even for Americans who don't associate it with the word.

The ordinary use of the term, however, probably rests more on a confusion between statistical norms and evaluative norms. An evaluative norm is a standard, a criterion of value. It is radically different from any question that statistics could answer, since it may well be that the normative standard in sex is not normally attained; or it may be that there are different normative standards. Yet in matters of sex, people mistakenly suppose that the statistical norm must reveal the standard of healthy sexuality. Why is this?

The best answer to this question was supplied by a historian of medical science named Georges Canguilhem. In his book *The Normal and the Pathological,* Canguilhem argues that modern medicine has been based on a confusion about the normal, ever since it first began using statistics. He shows that for the early-nineteenth-century Belgian statistician Lambert Adolphe Quételet, the study of averages proved the existence of intrinsic regularity: "For me the principal idea is to cause the truth to prevail and to show how much man, without his knowledge, is subject to divine laws and with what regularity he realizes them." The statistical norm, in other words, was seen by Quételet as evidence of divine law. As

descriptive vs evaluative norm

doctors began using Quételet's statistical methods, they usually thought they were discovering natural laws, rather than divine ones, but the effect was the same: normal came to mean right, proper, healthy. What most people are, the new wisdom went, is what people should be. If we can find through enough figures what the normal range is for, say, body temperature or blood pressure, then we can find out what body temperature or blood pressure should be. It seemed only a small and logical step, later in the nineteenth century, to extend the same thinking to sexuality. What most people do or desire is, according to the new science, what people should do and desire. It is this kind of thinking that leads people to buy copies of *Sexual Behavior in the Human Male* or *Sex in America,* hoping to find that their own sex lives conform to the norm.

The trouble is that the thinking was flawed from the outset. Not only was it a mistake to apply the medical ideal of a single health state to human sexuality, as though one sexuality were the right and healthy standard for everyone; it was a mistake to suppose that norms of health worked this way even for medical science. The idea of a biological norm, Canguilhem argues, is partly an expression of social norms. He offers the example of hypoglycemia, or blood sugar levels. African blacks, he notes, have lower rates of glycemia than Europeans; the difference is thought to correspond to different standards of activity. Given these conditions, who decides what level of glycemia will be classified as hypoglycemia— that is, as pathological? "If the European can serve as a norm, it is only to the extent that his kind of life will be able to pass as normative" (172). Changes in human physiology over time, in different natural environments, and in different kinds of society suggest that "the abnormal of today" is "the normal of yesterday" (174).

Canguilhem is no simple relativist. Nor is he trying to get us to reject all norms. His key thesis is that health should not be defined as a correspondence to a single norm laid down as a natural law of the species; rather, it is "the capacity to establish other norms in other conditions" (183). Variations from the norm, in other words, are not necessarily signs of pathology. They can become new norms. They are even necessary for health in this higher sense. The question of what is right or healthy is something that cannot be answered simply by natural laws of the biological organism. In matters of health, it depends partly on what conditions people live in, what their way of life is, and what they are willing to tolerate or aspire to. "Man feels in good health—which is health itself—only when he feels more than normal—that is, adapted to the environment and its demands—but normative, capable of following new norms of life. . . . To paraphrase a saying of Valéry, we have said that the possible abuse of health is part of health" (200). Health requires variation, not a pregiven norm.

If this is true of physiology and health, how much more easily could it be said in matters of sex, which lie so close to individuals' sense of health, freedom, and aspiration? How did we ever come to accept a world in which we are told to have a certain sexuality just because it is the average of a large population? Or, for that matter, because it is said to be the natural functioning of the human organism? One reason for the current vogue of evolutionary biology is that it seems to provide this kind of justification for heterosexuality, finding ways that it can be seen as adapted to the survival of the species. I suspect that most work in this field is committed to this story from the outset and is finding what it wants to find. Even if such hypotheses were correct, Canguilhem's argument should lead us to say: so what? If reproductive coupling served some evolutionary interests for early *Homo sapiens,* and could therefore have been called normal to those functions, it remains the case that health lies not in the repetition of those functions for all persons or for all time, but in the ability to create new functions, new adaptations, new conditions. It is even more surprising that gay people could be persuaded to accept such a notion, since homosexuality was for so long the classic example of abnormal and pathological sexuality. From the late nineteenth century onward, people had to work very hard to resist this medical fallacy, which was rooted in the confusion between statistical regularities and natural laws. The lesson in this struggle should have been one of skepticism toward all norms of health that express social norms, preferences for certain ways of living, or the tastes of a majority. And for many activists, that remains one of the principal lessons in the history of the lesbian and gay movement.

So it is ironic, to say the least, when we are now told that our aspiration should be to see ourselves as normal. No doubt gay people regard this as the ultimate answer to the common implication that being gay is pathological. No, they want to insist, we're normal. But this is to buy into a false alternative. The church tells us that our choice is to be saved or be damned; but of course it might be that these are not the only options, any more than Democrat and Republican need be the only options in politics. Just so, normal and pathological are not the only options. One of the reasons why so many people have started using the word "queer" is that it is a way of saying: "We're not pathological, but don't think for that reason that we want to be normal." People who are defined by a variant set of norms commit a kind of social suicide when they begin to measure the worth of their relations and their way of life by the yardstick of normalcy. The history of the movement should have taught us to ask: whose norm?

The politics of normal is the newest form of the drama of ambivalence that has marked gay politics since the Mattachine Society. On one hand, it seems like the perfect response to sexual shame. What could be a better way of legitimating oneself than to insist on being seen as normal? The problem, always, is that embracing this standard merely throws shame on those who stand farther down the ladder of respectability. It does not seem to be possible to think of oneself as normal without thinking that some other kind of person is pathological. What could have been seen as healthy variation is now seen as deviance. The rhetoric of normalization also tells us that the taken-for-granted norms of common sense are the only criteria of value. Rival views become unimaginable by this standard. So just as isolation, privatization, and obviousness have the effect of coercion in the politics of shame, so does the idealization of the normal.

The embrace of normal is also a prime example of antipolitical politics. The point of being normal is to blend, to have no visible difference and no conflict. Sullivan's *Virtually Normal* claimed that gay politics reduced to only two issues: military service and marriage. Everything else is mere private difference. If you are queer and don't want to enlist or get a marriage license, then politics is not for you. The message, which Sullivan later took to gay audiences in promoting his *Same-Sex Marriage: Pro and Con,* is that the lesbian and gay movement is essentially over, or will be when gay couples can marry. This message goes over well with a key constituency: middle-class white gay men, many of whom were never happy to be political, anyway. It turns the lesbian and gay movement into a project for divorcing homosexuality first from sex and then from politics. Sullivan has the candor and consistency to follow this line of thinking to its conclusion. "Following legalization of same-sex marriage and a couple of

other things," he has declared, "I think we should have a
party and close down the gay rights movement for good."
Naturally, many activists get cold feet at this point in the
chain of reasoning, considering that the culture continues to
be as homophobic as it is.

Sullivan's argument was an extreme instance of both of the
long-term tensions that I see running throughout the history
of lesbian and gay politics: identity ambivalence and the lure
of the normal. In retrospect, I would say that it also marked
something new. In 1993, Sullivan's *New Republic* manifesto
could only be read as a contentious provocation, consistent
with his enfant terrible persona. But that was in 1993. Now,
only a few years later, the ideal of homosexuals without sex
underlying Sullivan's argument circulates in many quarters as
mere common sense. It presents itself no longer as con-
tentiousness, but as the happy valley beyond contention.
Now a desexed magazine like *Hero* can claim to be "the magazine for the rest of us," without seeming to be provocative or
political at all.

THE NORMALIZED MOVEMENT

At a public forum in New York in the summer of 1998, James
Collard, the newly appointed editor of *Out* magazine, announced what he took to be a new dawn in the lesbian and
gay movement. Having begun his editorship by taking the
words "gay and lesbian" off the cover of the magazine, he was
ready, he told the audience, to declare himself "post-gay."
(Larry Kramer had recently embraced the same label in *The
Advocate*.) The theory behind the term remained vague, at
best, but clearly it had nothing to do with being queer. For
Collard it had to do with being defined by "more than sexuality," with being critical of a "gay ghetto" and the clone style

fostered there, and with recognizing that many gay people "no longer see their lives solely in terms of struggle." Citing his own preference for "mixed" clubs over gay or lesbian bars and clubs, Collard argued that "anger no longer has the power to unite us," that most gay people "are unlikely to be united by the orthodox tactics of angry veterans from earlier battles."

The audience at this forum was not convinced. As Collard's fellow panelist Kendall Thomas pointed out, no one would say that the appearance of some racially mixed club settings or the rise of a black bourgeosie or the appearance of one black sitcom in any way meant that African Americans are now free to be "post-black." Why did the limited gains of some lucky gay people mean that we were suddenly "post-gay"? Moreover, the narrative Collard took for granted rang false. Since when had anyone said that anger was the only valid gay emotion, or the only uniting force even in the angriest days of ACT UP? Since when had anyone lived "solely in terms of struggle"? When was being queer ever *only* about sexuality? What could be the point of saying these things if not implicitly to reshape the image of gay culture for the happy consumers of a lifestyle magazine like *Out?* Faced with a barrage of criticism, Collard simply retorted that the urban New York audience was out of touch with American gays and lesbians, that the people who were likely to be in sympathy with his "post-gay" views were not likely to show up at a public forum. They were likely to be home, making dinner for their boyfriends.

Here, at least, he was exactly right. Post-gay rhetoric appeals to those gay men and lesbians who were least happy to be political in the first place, who have enough of a safe place in the world—thanks in part to past struggle—to think of their own lives no longer in terms of struggle. Magazines like

Out make it possible for large numbers of gay people to see themselves this way and to feel that they take part in something called "the gay community" without needing to belong to a political scene. For Collard, that is all to the good.

The rest of us, meanwhile, might wonder if there are other reasons why gay people prefer to stay home these days. When Collard says that "anger no longer has the power to unite us," he would seem to be right. Apart from the much-publicized example of Matthew Shepard's murder in 1998, very little seems to have the power to animate gay people now. They're home, making dinner for their boyfriends, and that's as united as they're going to get. It is no mere nostalgia to notice that not long ago, in the so-called ghettos it is now so fashionable to disdain, word about a new and dangerous development could travel with electric speed, and a crowd could materialize with a common will at almost no notice, not only at Stonewall, but repeatedly for more than twenty years afterward. Instant protests, for example, arose upon news of the shooting of the homophobic film *Cruising* in 1979; the same thing happened after a number of waves of police entrapments and harassments in the '70s and '80s; and again when realization of a health crisis sank in in the '80s. The most famous of these were events of great anger, such as the riots in San Francisco following the trial of Dan White for killing Harvey Milk, or several years later in Los Angeles after Governor Pete Wilson vetoed a gay rights bill. People could also materialize for events of public mourning or celebration. A public could be mobilized for electioneering, for partying, or for developing a wide-ranging response to a health crisis.

It is difficult to imagine many circumstances that could produce the same public manifestation now. There are just as many occasions of danger now as ever before. Police entrap men in parks and bathrooms just as they did in 1950. They close gay bars now as they did in the 1960s. Sodomy laws remain on the books and repeal efforts have all but stalled. Politicians defund AIDS services and reject public health counsel in favor of moralism now as they did in the 1980s. New health hazards arise, while the health activism movement that responded to AIDS crumbles. And people stay home. Collard thinks they are voting with their feet. Perhaps it is true that they stay home because they believe, like Collard, that the time has come when "they can live their lives freely and openly." Perhaps their memory of stigma is short. Perhaps they are simply tired and disillusioned about a movement that no longer seems to aspire to changing much. Perhaps they have learned that the movement has its own mass and inertia, and no longer believe that they have much say in it. Whatever the reason, they stay home.

Collard, though, had another response to those of his critics who did not stay home, one that was far more effective. Unable to make a convincing case to the crowd, he took his complaint directly to the pages of *Newsweek*. There it ran under the headline "LEAVING THE GAY GHETTO," accompanying a cover story on "ex-gays," the fundamentalist crusade to "cure" people of being queer. In this new context, Collard got to portray himself as a brave freedom fighter: "I called for a new post-gay identity, defined by more than sexuality and more open to self-criticism. So I got criticized—a lot." He implied that, just by showing up at the meeting, these urban queers were not representative of the new tide in the gay movement. He even compared himself to the members of South Africa's African National Congress, praising them for having the courage of self-criticism and faulting his New York audience for not doing the same.

This was great PR. At least as long as no one noticed that Collard was not doing "self-criticism." He was criticizing other people, not himself. And his terms seemed designed to appeal to no one so much as straight readers: the only visible features of a critique were an implicit devaluation of sexuality, disdain for "the gay ghetto," an explanation of gay male clone style as a pathological "obsession," and a relegation of gay politics to the dark and archaic past of "angry veterans from earlier battles," with their PC conformity and "orthodox tactics." But this is not a self-criticism. It's hostile stereotype.

Collard did no better, in this new context, at defining "post-gay." He called it "simply a critique of gay politics and gay culture—by gay people, for gay people." Lost, apparently, was the irony of making this claim on the pages of *Newsweek*—hardly a magazine written "by gay people, for gay people." Nor did Collard manage to say what his "critique" was, except the stereotypes he was so ready to trot out as new insight. It's not a critique to say that gay male clones are "obsessed" with their bodies. They will tell you that themselves. It's not a critique to say that the "gay ghetto" can be homogeneous and shallow. That remark is made, shallowly, at nearly every dinner party in Chelsea or on Fire Island. If you really wanted an example of self-criticism, you would do better to turn to the pages of *Out of the Closets,* the classic 1972 collection of writings from the heady days of gay liberation, now dismissed by Collard as an antiquated orthodoxy but displaying a range of views and emotions that *Out* magazine and its counterparts have never rivaled.

Collard's "post-gay" narrative, in fact, is a dressed-up version of the same rhetoric that sounds so quaint when quoted from the Mattachine Society's papers. Then and now, homosexuals were and still are afraid to be seen as queer. Then and now, they knew and still know that nothing else could haunt their attempt to be "ethical," in the restricted sense that prevails in America, as much as sex. Then as now, they bargained and still bargain for a debased pseudo-dignity, the kind that is awarded as a bribe for disavowing the indignity of sex and the double indignity of a politics around sex. The result has always been a set of hierarchies. Those whose sex is least threatening, along with those whose gender profiles seem least queer, are put forward as the good and acceptable face of the movement. These, inevitably, are the ones who are staying home, making dinner for their boyfriends, for whom being gay means reading *Newsweek*. The others, the queers who have sex in public toilets, who don't "come out" as happily gay, the sex workers, the lesbians who are too vocal about a taste for dildos or S/M, the boys who flaunt it as pansies or as leathermen, the androgynes, the trannies or transgendered whose gender deviance makes them unassimilable to the menu of sexual orientations, the clones in the so-called gay ghetto, the fist-fuckers and popper-snorters, the ones who actually like pornography—all these flaming creatures are told, in an earnestness that betrays no glimmer of its own grotesque comedy, that their great moment of liberation and acceptance will come later, when we "no longer see our lives solely in terms of struggle," when we get to be about "more than sexuality"—when, say, gay marriage is given the force of law. Free at last!

This betrayal of the abject and the queer in favor of a banalized respectability does not result, in my view, from malice. Many of the people who are setting priorities in the lesbian and gay movement honestly believe in a rainbow coalition, or in trickle-down acceptance. Collard may well be one of these. But his language implicitly desexualizes the movement and depoliticizes queer sex. This move will always create a hierarchy, whether it is intended to or not, but one that goes without a name because it is not based on identity. It is not overtly a hatred for a distinct class of persons. It manifests itself usually as a benign distinction between identity and sex. The effect is a kind of expulsion, abjection, and contempt for those more visibly defined by sex, and this effect is all the more powerful for its apparent innocuousness. Very often, but not always, it will reinforce other hierarchies of respectability—those of gender deviance, of race, of work and class, of urban geography. But it is harder for those who suffer from it to fight back. It's especially hard to fight when it comes from the very people who are in the business of defending one's gay or lesbian identity.

The queer ethos is currently thriving in urban scenes, in pockets of alternative culture in the suburbs, among younger queers, in drag culture, among black and Latino cultures, in club scenes and the arts, on web sites and in queer zines, among all kinds of people in the least likely places. For all this vitality, it is no longer the public face of the lesbian and gay movement. It does find expression in many local organizations: health service organizations, community centers, motorcycle clubs, theater groups, churches, antiviolence campaigns, transgender alliances, racial or ethnic groups, private support groups—you name it. But this immense network, in which so many people are working to bring a queer world into being, is less and less what people have in mind when they think of the lesbian and gay movement. Over the past decade, movement politics on the national scale has been dramatically transformed. Its public face is now dominated by a small group of national organizations, an equally small group of media celebrities, connected to a network of big-money politics that revolves around publicity consultants and campaign professionals and litigators. The new conditions of movement politics have vastly heightened the tensions that have simmered in the movement since the Mattachine Society, increasing the tendency to present the movement in terms oriented to the dominant culture. Worse, the public face of the lesbian and gay movement is increasingly determined not in queer counterpublics at all, but on the pages of *Newsweek*. The most visible spokespersons of the lesbian and gay movement—and on the pages of *Newsweek*, certainly, Collard's views are not challenged—have increasingly bought into the going assumption about who gets to "accept" whom, along with an equally false antinomy between dignity and sex. In doing so they have redefined the movement and its constituency. Between the thriving scenes of minor queer counterpublics and the more visible world of the official lesbian and gay movement, a gap has been widening that leaves people on each side staring in incomprehension and distaste.

When someone like Collard trumps his skeptical urban audience by taking his post-gay rhetoric to the pages of *Newsweek*, he finds the environment where it will resonate most powerfully with the everyday assumptions of the straight culture. It allows Collard to flex the prosthetic muscles of mass-mediated opinion and its version of common sense. In the pages of *Newsweek*, what could be more self-evident than distaste for the "gay ghetto"? What could be more self-evidently foreign than seeing one's life in terms of struggle? Given this kind of common sense, one would be hard pressed to imagine the other side of the picture.

What is most destructive, in my view, is not simply the contradiction inherent in Collard's rhetoric, which in itself is hardly new, but rather the newfound ability of respectable gay people to project themselves as the true lesbian and gay movement, and thus to trump those queers who do not share their own sense of the world. There always seem to be some gay men and lesbians willing to denounce gay culture from the safe perch of the straight media. They regard this as a sign of courage and nonconformity, and they think that their ability to find such a large audience is evidence of their superior reasoning, or the natural popularity of their views among gay people. But nothing could be farther from the truth. Their power derives from the stigmaphobe context in which they speak: from mass-mediated publics, institutions of law and the state, concentrations of money in politics, the structure of national organizations, and the privatization of public space.

A mass medium like *Newsweek* has its own gravity. As part of the total package of mass culture, it continually addresses us as normal. Its editors and writers know that they have to present the world in familiar terms to as many people as possible. The more people who can recognize themselves in its pages, the more money the magazine makes. We are invited to measure ourselves against the rest of the population, with its deviations and extremes, and to make sure that we fit within this range along with all the other normals. We are provided with a constant backdrop of polling, reportage on popular tastes and trends, sales figures from the mass media, and guesses about the mass of public opinion. Reading *Newsweek* we become, if temporarily, that fictional creature, the *Newsweek* reader. And the *Newsweek* reader is nothing if not normal. The function of *Newsweek* is to tell normal people about all the things that are not normal, since normal people like *Newsweek*'s readers would not know otherwise. Out there, we eagerly learn, there are deviations such as the "gay ghetto." These are not just mere differences, or variations, because no matter how much we think we value individuality, we also believe that there is a kind of natural law to the range of averages. It is normal to be normal. The kind of consciousness one has of the world in mass culture, in other words, has a tendency to normalize us; that is, to make us aspire to be normal, to make us adjust our perceptions of ourselves and others, so that we fit within the common range.

At the same time, mass media like *Newsweek* have their own way of connecting people. They reach private individuals in their intimate spaces, in order to connect consumers directly to the global world of mass culture. We think we are being given solidarity with the world and do not notice that this imaginary commonality is in fact a substitute for the very kind of active, public solidarity of which we are so acutely deprived.

Collard's argument was perfectly adapted to both of these tendencies in mass media. It addressed readers who want to be normal, out of the gay ghetto, defined by "more than sexuality." And it addressed readers who are united with one another neither by sex nor by anger, still less by politics and the orthodox tactics of veteran activists, but rather by staying home and reading magazines. As the gay and lesbian movement comes to be more and more at home in the environment of mass media, it suffers from both of these tendencies. It makes us imagine that we want to be normal. And it makes us imagine that by consuming mass images of gay people we somehow belong completely to the wider world, even while we stay at home and make dinner for our boyfriends. Instead of taking part in a queer movement, we become part of a gay trend.

When you begin interacting with people in queer culture, by contrast, you unlearn that perspective. You learn that everyone deviates from the norm in some context or other, and that the statistical norm has no moral value. You begin to recognize how stultifying the faith in the norm can be. You learn that the people who look most different from you can be, by virtue of that fact, the very people from whom you have the most to learn. Your lot is cast with them, and you begin to recognize that there are other worlds of interaction that the mass media cannot comprehend, worlds that they can only deform when they project images of ghettos and other deviant scenes. To seek out queer culture, to interact with it and learn from it, is a kind of public activity. It is a way of transforming oneself, and at the same time helping to elaborate a commonly accessible world.

The difference between Collard's views and those of his audience in New York, in short, amounts to more than a mere difference of opinion or an argument with two sides. It represents a difference between two worlds. One, the world of mass media and their quasi-official politics, is immensely powerful—so much so that it can make us forget what this other world is like. In this book I am trying to point out the way current conflicts within the gay and lesbian movement, especially debates about public sex and marriage, are not so much debates with shared assumptions as points of conflict and miscomprehension between increasingly divergent worlds.

This difference has become the most important fault line in the movement. It is widely misrecognized. A variety of labels have been tried out in recent years to explain the growing conflict, and they all prove to be misleading. Writing in the *New York Times*, the reporter Adam Nagourney interprets the conflict as one between pragmatists and . . . something that Nagourney can't even find a label for. He calls them "two major forces that have roiled the gay rights movement over the decades," in an epic "struggle between pragmatic homosexuals who seek to work with government and more hostile advocates who tend to view government as an enemy." This is fairly tendentious language for a gay journalist to use in the paper of record. He would have us believe that on one side are pragmatism, compromise, and successful politics; on the other, "street firebrands" and people "who want to throw rocks through the window."

Ironically, one of the occasions of Nagourney's article was the endorsement, in the 1998 elections, of New York Senator Alfonse D'Amato by the most prominent national gay organization, the Human Rights Campaign. I say "ironically" because the endorsement was neither pragmatic nor successful. D'Amato lost, in part because the gay vote went against him by a 3 to 1 margin. So the HRC managed to alienate not only the vast majority of gay people in New York, but also the incoming senator. Pragmatism in gay politics requires some sense of principle, and some accountability to gays and lesbians. The Human Rights Campaign, in endorsing D'Amato, showed neither. HRC, in fact, has no very great record of success to boast about compared to other gay groups, and by Nagourney's own account its "determined pragmatism" consists mainly in "a policy of picking the incumbent." But when the incumbent has, even by HRC's standards, a significantly lower rating on gay issues than his opponent, when he has as well the worst record on AIDS of the entire New York delegation, when he has been consistently against reproductive choice, when he has pandered to the far right by attacking gay and lesbian artists funded by the NEA, when he has contributed to Republican stonewalling on countless other issues, when he is roundly detested by the New York gay voters who know best of his record and his profile within the state, endorsing him shows an odd definition of pragmatism. And what of the other side on this question? Can the *New York Times* really discern nothing more than a desire to throw rocks? If that were the only alternative, then *Hero's* appeal to "the rest of us" would be sensible, indeed.

It is often said that the difference is one between left and right. Some media figures, such as Andrew Sullivan and author Bruce Bawer, have indeed avowed a fairly conservative vision. They routinely denounce their foes as antiquated lefties. Their foes, in turn, have denounced them as right-wingers and have argued for a liberal or radical left vision of queer politics. I make no secret of my sympathies with the latter, but the central issues—at least for this book—are not just left/right, liberal/conservative, centrist/radical. It is easy enough to find people on the right who think that neither the government nor the moralists have any business interfering with uncoerced sex. And the left for its part has a long puritanical tradition dating at least from, well, the Puritans (who counted among their radicals the divorce agitator John Milton). Political philosophy is not a very good predictor of sexual ethic, nor vice versa.

Within the context of the gay and lesbian movement, "left" and "right" are given a rather special usage, in which "left" means pro-sex and right means anti-sex. This, too, is misleading shorthand. The implication tends to be that those who favor sex, especially casual sex, are opposed by those who favor romantic love. But queer culture is the last place where this opposition should be taken for granted. One of its greatest contributions to modern life is the discovery that you can have both: intimacy and casualness; long-term commitment and sex with strangers; romantic love and perverse pleasure. To cast the conflict as one between sex and love is to deny the best insights and lived experience of queers. Moreover, if casual sex and romantic love seem like two distinct options, is one leftist and the other conservative? Would I have to break up with my lover in order to be radical or queer? Would a conservative need to be in a couple in order to be conservative? Right-leaning gays often claim that their critics are opposed to love. And left-leaning gays often claim that their critics are opposed to sex. But both claims distort the issue. As I argued in the last chapter, you do not have to believe that all sex is good or happy or redemptive in order to argue that we should challenge the politics of sexual shame. And similarly, those who advocate sexual shaming usually believe, or claim to believe, that sex (theoretically) is good.

Matters are not much helped by the distinction between assimilation and separatism. This is probably the most familiar way of understanding the conflict. The problem is that hardly anyone admits to being either an assimilationist or a separatist. And like the conflict between left and right, it doesn't tell us as much about the politics of sex as it might seem. You could certainly be separatist on grounds other than sex. You could believe, for example, in gay sensibility, or fairy spirituality, or sisterhood. Any of these could separate us (or some of us) from straight culture. You could also be assimilationist and claim to appreciate sex as long as it takes place in the "proper" way—in private, in perspective, under control. Either way, as a separatist or as an assimilationist, you could expect gay and lesbian politics to be about identity, not sex; status, not conduct; persons, not acts.

On the other hand, the politics I advocate—a frank embrace of queer sex in all its apparent indignity, together with a frank challenge to the damaging hierarchies of respectability—can result in neither assimilation nor separatism if carried through consistently. Against assimilation, one could insist that the dominant culture assimilate to queer culture, not the other way around. Straight culture has already learned much from queers, and it shouldn't stop now. In particular, it needs to learn a new standard of dignity, and it won't do this as long as gay people think that their "acceptance" needs to be won on the terms of straight culture's politics of shame.

Does this position result in separatism? Quite the contrary. Were we to recognize the diversity of what we call sexuality with the kind of empathic realism in which many queers are unsurpassed, the result would not be separatism, and could not be, because it would give us no view of who "we" are apart from the fact that there are a lot of nonnormative sexualities in the world. This possibility has been voiced by queer writers of the past, from Walt Whitman through Jean Genet, and by contemporary critics as different as Pat Califia and Eve Sedgwick—who are neither separatists nor assimilationists. The frank refusal to repudiate sex or the undignified people who have it, which I see as the tacit or explicit ethos in countless scenes of queer culture, is the antithesis of identity politics.

I believe that this difference in ethical orientation, a difference in ways of resolving the ambivalence of stigma, best explains the political divisions in the movement now. In part we may be seeing a shift over time from stigmaphile to stigmaphobe politics. Those who fought the earliest struggles of the movement were those least cowed by shame. Their very success has allowed others to see themselves as part of a movement without having to take the same degree of risk. That may be a good thing in itself, but its unanticipated result is that many of the newer arrivals to the movement are less disposed to challenge the force of shame and stigma fully. In some cases, they now think the movement should belong to them. Some display no sense of the movement's history at all, while others dismiss that history as a stage of immaturity. They claim to be more moral, more advanced, more pragmatic. By understanding the dynamics of stigma and identity ambivalence we can see that there is an element of self-serving cant in this story. The new respectability of lesbian and gay politics is not the movement's coming of age; it is, in effect, a takeover. The lower threshold of defiance required for entry into the movement now means that the balance of power within it has shifted from the stigmaphile to the stigmaphobe poles. And this does not mean a gain of integrity, but a loss.

In other ways, though, the changing profile of the movement has to do not only with this dynamic over time, but with the surrounding context of American culture in the Clinton era. The difference in ethos is accentuated by underlying factors: especially the heavy capitalization of national politics, the environment of mass culture, and the corporate organizational structure of some national groups such as the HRC. Behind the desexualization of the lesbian and gay movement and the depoliticization of queer sex in the 1990s, I think we can see at least the following distinct but related developments:

- the changed nature of the AIDS epidemic, from one understood as crisis to one understood as a chronic, manageable problem;
- the decline of direct-action activism;
- the loss of political memory that attended so many deaths in a culture with few institutions of memory;
- the 1992 election and the appearance of Clintonian politics on the national scene;
- the growing importance of big-money election campaigns and lobbying;
- the consequent prominence of a fat-cat donor base within the movement, often consisting of well-heeled men with very little lived connection to the most despised parts of the queer world;
- the growing centralization of gay politics by national organizations headquartered in Washington;
- the appeal of a "place at the table" notion that what

we really wanted was to be represented—either by
officials or by celebrities—rather than to belong actively to a movement;

• the rise of highly capitalized lifestyle magazines as the
principal public venue of the movement;

• the consequent rise of a politics of media celebrity, in
which a handful of gay pundits selected within the
media system dominate opinion making;

• and the extraordinary success of some of those pundits in promoting a neoliberal (that is, neoconservative) spin on what the movement is about.

Almost all of these new conditions came into alignment in
the early 1990s. Before 1990, for example, the gay press consisted mostly of local community newspapers. *The Advocate*, a
news weekly, was the dominant national magazine, along
with the semi-intellectual *Out/Look*. In some periodicals, no-
tably *The Body Politic* and *Gay Community News*, you could
find serious, innovative thought alongside news coverage.
Both these magazines were especially good at keeping up an
awareness of the earlier movement's legacies. Both folded,
and slick lifestyle magazines rose up in their place. Most of
the new magazines—*Genre, Out, XY, Girlfriends*, and many
others—are national, and they soon began attracting mainstream advertisers. Whatever their undoubted attractions
(may they all thrive), and despite the best intentions of the
people working on them, this generation of magazines by
their very nature could not substitute for the lost forums of
debate.

At about the same time, the national organizations realigned themselves. The Human Rights Campaign, founded
in 1980 as a political action committee for channeling money
to gay and gay-friendly candidates, built up its donor base so

well that by 1988 its budget was twice that of its rival, the National Gay and Lesbian Task Force. Though it began as a low-profile group whose very name (then the Human Rights Campaign Fund) provided cover for closeted donors and skittish candidates, by 1993 HRC had become an extensive organization with a high public profile, an active policy role, and a major lobbying investment. It has now far eclipsed all rivals as the most visible organ of lesbian and gay politics. Its budget for fiscal year 1999 is 15.1 million dollars—three times that of 1995. (But still mere pennies compared to its right-wing counterparts.) Its policies are determined by a corporate-style national board, and the lion's share of the money has always come from well-to-do (mostly male) donors. That, of course, is no crime, and one can easily regard HRC's donors and board members as worthy people working on laudable projects. The fact remains that the organization differs in kind from the groups that preceded it and that continue to be the infrastructure of politics at the local level.

These smaller groups have less money and less visibility but more direct accountability to those they claim to represent. You can get to a leadership role in them without being rich, without belonging to an elite, and without attending a black-tie fund-raiser. For these structural reasons, and not because of anyone's moral intentions, they are more likely to be permeated by a queer ethos. HRC, by contrast, is oriented to the stigmaphobe world not just in ethos but in structure. Respectability is the goal of its politics because respectability is the prerequisite for being heard within it. Its increasing ability to project itself as the voice of the movement, therefore, skews the meaning of gay politics. Even the smaller groups find themselves changing course accordingly, as they are now overshadowed in national politics, in fund-raising, and in media visibility.

And each of the developments I've listed reinforces the others. The national magazines and HRC, for example, address their constituencies in relatively similar ways. And their tendency to normalize the movement finds greater expression because neither has many serious rivals for moral leadership. In previous years an organization such as HRC, though not structurally accountable to anyone, might at least have needed to answer more to thoughtful veterans of movement politics. Those voices have now been eclipsed. The emergent spokespersons of the movement are a different and much more visible group of people: the columnists of the lifestyle magazines along with a small number of writers and celebrities of the straight press. Their prominence comes from conditions that have almost nothing to do with the scenes of queer culture. Hollywood actors come out one day and are icons of the movement the next. And professional columnists, however admirable they might be individually, are constrained by the need to maintain their own notoriety, which in the circular system of media culture is the basis of their celebrity and the main reason that they are listened to in the first place. These conditions do not produce the kind of critical public dialogue that movement politics thrives on. They produce a potent simulacrum of a movement.

To the national audience of the United States, it may seem that the gay movement is more visible and powerful than ever. To queers on the ground, this monumental appearance feels as fake as the marbleized façades of 1990s corporate architecture. People know, even if they cannot pinpoint the reasons, that it is an alien will that finds expression there. They shrug, or they complain, and it doesn't matter; gay politics goes on without them. Under the new conditions of the Clinton era, long-simmering tensions between a politics of homosexuality and a politics of sex have taken a newly destructive form. At its best, queer politics has fought the stigmatization of sex, in all the ramifications that stigma has for people, from queer youth to sex workers and single mothers. But in its newest manifestation, the lesbian and gay movement threatens to become an instrument for the normalization of queer life. Nowhere is that more visible than in the presentation of the gay marriage issue.

CHAPTER THREE
BEYOND GAY MARRIAGE

*"There are no societies which do not regulate sex, and thus all
societies create the hope of escaping from such regulations."*
—*Michel Foucault, 1973*

In 1996, debating the so-called Defense of Marriage
Act in the House of Representatives, Illinois Republican
Henry Hyde delivered what he thought was a clinching argument against same-sex marriage: "People don't think that
the traditional marriage ought to be demeaned or trivialized
by same-sex unions." Massachusetts Democratic Congress-
man Barney Frank quickly seized on what seemed a careless
phrase. "How does it demean your marriage? If other people
are immoral, how does it demean your marriage?" Hyde,
who was later forced to admit an adulterous affair even as he
came to head the Republican prosecution in the Clinton impeachment, could not manage much of an answer. "It de-
means the institution," he said, lamely. "My marriage was
never demeaned. The institution of marriage is trivialized by
same-sex marriage."

The thing that makes Hyde's remark wrong—not just illogical or pompous—is that it becomes a program not for his own sexuality, but for someone else's. He doesn't just want his marriage to be holy; he wants it to be holy *at the expense of someone else's.* To see gay marriage as "demeaning" is, in his view, a way of seeing "traditional marriage" as more significant. Barney Frank and other marriage advocates have only to expose such thinking to the ridicule it deserves in order to point up its injustice.

But the invidiousness of Hyde's remark is a feature of marriage, not just *straight* marriage. Marriage sanctifies some couples at the expense of others. It is selective legitimacy. This is a necessary implication of the institution, and not just the result of bad motives or the high-toned non sequiturs of Henry Hyde. To a couple that gets married, marriage just looks ennobling, as it does to Hyde. Stand outside it for a second and you see the implication: if you don't have it, you and your relations are less worthy. Without this corollary effect, marriage would not be able to endow anybody's life with significance. The ennobling and the demeaning go together. Marriage does one only by virtue of the other. Marriage, in short, discriminates.

That is one reason why same-sex marriage provokes such powerful outbursts of homophobic feeling in many straight people, when they could just as easily view marriage as the ultimate conformity of gay people to their own norms. They want marriage to remain a privilege, a mark that they are special. Often they are willing to grant all (or nearly all) the benefits of marriage to gay people, as long as they don't have to give up the word "marriage." They need some token, however magical, of superiority. But what about the gay people who want marriage? Would they not in turn derive their sense of pride from the invidious and shaming distinction between the married and the unmarried?

It must be admitted from the outset that there is something unfashionable, and perhaps untimely, about any discussion of marriage as a goal in gay politics. One is apt to feel like the unmannerly wedding guest, gossiping about divorce at the rehearsal dinner. At this point the only people arguing against gay marriage, it seems, are those homophobic dinosaurs—like Hyde, or Senator Jesse Helms, or the feminist philosopher Jean Bethke Elshtain—who still think that marriage is about procreation, or that same-sex marriage somehow threatens to "tear apart America's moral fabric," as Helms put it on the Senate floor. Pope John Paul II is reported to have claimed that same-sex marriage "is a serious threat to the future of the family and society itself." If the arguments against gay marriage are as silly and phobic as this, then naturally marrying will seem to strike deep against bigotry. What purpose could be served by a skeptical discussion of marriage now, given the nature of the opposition?

None at all, says Evan Wolfson, director of the Marriage Project at the Lambda Legal Defense and Education Fund. Wolfson argues that in the wake of *Baehr v. Lewin*—the Hawaii Supreme Court decision that appeared to pave the way for gay marriage—we should "end, or at least suspend, the intra-community debate over whether to seek marriage. The ship has sailed." He cites the need for a united front against the wave of homophobic state and national initiatives designed to wed marriage indissolubly to heterosexuality. As he also points out, there is ample room for foolishness or hubris when intellectuals ask, at this date, whether or not gay marriage is a worthy political cause. The decision is no longer up to us. The legal system of the United States has its own momentum. The last thing the courts are likely to care about is whether marriage is a good idea from a queer point of view.

There is a kernel of truth in this. One has only to pop the question—for or against gay marriage?—to find oneself at once irrelevant to a process that is no longer a debate, blinded by the urgent temporality of the headline, and suckered into a phony plebiscite. But on this, as on so much else, it may be the courts that will prove to have the narrow view. Within the context that Wolfson takes for granted, dissent is indeed almost unheard. Since the 1993 March on Washington, marriage has come to dominate the political imagination of the national gay movement in the United States. To read the pages of *The Advocate* or *Out* is to receive the impression that gay people hardly care about anything else, other than entertainment. I have no doubt that a large constituency has been formed around this belief. But the commitment is not universally shared, to put it mildly. Gay men, lesbians, and many other unmarried people on the street are just as likely to be made slightly sick by the topic, or perhaps to shrug it off as yet another example of that weird foreign language that people speak in the media world of politics, policy, and punditry.

No one was more surprised by the rise of the gay marriage issue than many veterans of earlier forms of gay activism. To them, marriage seems both less urgent and less agreed upon than such items as HIV and health care, AIDS prevention, the repeal of sodomy laws, antigay violence, job discrimination, immigration, media coverage, military antigay policy, sex inequality, and the saturation of everyday life by heterosexual privilege. Before the election of Bill Clinton in 1992, marriage was scarcely a visible blip on the horizon of queer politics; Paula Ettelbrick and Tom Stoddard's 1989 debate on the issue seemed, at the time, simply theoretical. Many gay activists abroad are equally baffled by the focus on marriage in the United States. To them, at least, it is hardly up to Americans to "suspend the intra-community debate." Both within the

United States and abroad, people have tried or discussed an immense array of other options—from common-law marriage and domestic partnership to the disentangling of health and other benefits from matrimony, to the Scandinavian model of a second-tier marriage (identical to straight marriage except for parenting rights), to the French model of legal concubinage, to the newer package of reforms known in France as the *pacte civil de solidarité* (PACS, a "civil solidarity pact" that bestows benefits on households of all kinds, including cohabiting siblings). Given this variety of alternatives, it may well strike many as odd that the question has suddenly been reduced to this: same-sex marriage, pro or con?

The time is ripe to reconsider the issue. The campaign for marriage, never a broad-based movement among gay and lesbian activists, depended for its success on the courts. It was launched by a relatively small number of lawyers, not by a consensus among activists. It remains a project of litigation, though now with the support of the major lesbian and gay organizations. So far the campaign has come up dry. After initial success with the Supreme Court of Hawaii in *Baehr v. Lewin,* advocates of same-sex marriage had reason to be optimistic. The tactic of legal advocacy had apparently worked. But outside the courtroom, the homophobic backlash was building. First, the so-called Defense of Marriage Act was passed by Congress and signed by President Clinton. Then, in November of 1998, a statewide referendum in Hawaii neutralized the *Baehr* decision by allowing the legislature to amend the constitution so as to restrict marriage to heterosexual couples. A similar measure passed in Alaska, and another is on the ballot for California in the year 2000. Moreover, the Hawaii vote was not even close. Though advocates of same-sex marriage had predicted an even battle, the final vote was nearly 70 percent to 30.

Are these merely stumbles in the progress of history? States are codifying restrictions on marriage that had merely been tacit custom before, making new obstacles to marriage reform for the future. Powerful antigay forces have been mobilized around the issue. If reform of marriage was the goal, the tactics of legal advocacy have not worked, and in some ways have made the problem worse. And if a reconsideration of the tactics seems to have been forced by this turn of events, it is also reasonable to reconsider the long-term strategic goal, since debate over the ultimate goals of reform was cut short by the turn to legal advocacy in the first place. "The ship has sailed," Wolfson confidently declared; but now that the ship has run aground, we might ask whether it was headed in the right direction.

How did the shift in an American national agenda come about? What will its consequences be? For whom would marriage be a victory? What would the value of gay marriage be, for example, to sexual dissidents who are not marrying couples? It is at least possible that the worst consequences would fall on those who did not recognize the question of gay marriage as an "intra-community debate" at all, but considered it as something foisted on them by fundamentally alien organizations. (It is no accident that the organizations promoting marriage are defined primarily as advocates for lesbian and gay identity rather than for nonnormative sexual cultures.) Where does the politics of gay marriage lead? What kind of marriage are we talking about, and how might its place in the larger context of state regulations about sexuality be changed? Behind the question of gay marriage as it is posed in the United States, these fundamental questions are not being aired. But they are the questions that count. We cannot wait until American courts have settled the marriage issue before addressing them, not least because the way they are answered will play a large part in determining the meaning and consequences of marriage.

MARRIAGE—WHY NOT?

Marriage became the dominant issue in lesbian and gay politics in the 1990s, but not before. If marriage is so fundamental to a program of rights, why did gay men and lesbians resist it over the twenty-five-year period of their most defiant activism? The issue had been raised from the beginning. In 1970, riding a burst of radical enthusiasm after Stonewall, the Reverend Troy Perry officiated a ceremony for two lesbians. Under California law at the time, common-law marriage could be formalized by a church ceremony after a couple had lived together for two years. (California law said nothing about the sexes of the couple.) The two women had lived together for just over two years, and so demanded (unsuccessfully, it turned out) that California recognize theirs as an already established common-law marriage. The same year, a gay male couple in Minnesota made national headlines by applying for a marriage license. One of the men, Jack Baker, wrote a lengthy rationale for what they had done. Baker emphasized that marriage was "used by the legal system as a distribution mechanism for many rights and privileges" and that as long as the culture considered marriage a right, it was necessary to demand it: "when any minority allows itself to be denied a right that is given to others, it is allowing itself to be relegated to a second-rate position." The mere posing of the issue was a jolt. It made the heterosexuality of marriage visible, to many people, for the first time. It drew attention to the exclusions entailed by marriage, through provisions for inheritance, wrongful death actions, tax rates, and the like. And it advanced a claim of equality that had undeniable appeal.

Baker's claims seemed scandalous to the straight press. They sparked animated discussions of theory and strategy within the groups that had organized in the wake of Stonewall.

Despite the strength of Baker's reasons, and despite the potent theatrical appeal of the issue, gay and lesbian groups did not pursue marriage as a central part of their strategy over the next twenty years. Why not? Was it simply a matter of lesbian resistance derived from the feminist critique of marriage? Were gay men just too busy snorting poppers at the baths? Was American culture simply not ready for gay marriage? These are the stories now being told by the advocates of same-sex marriage, back in the headlines after more than a quarter century. But we should not discount other explanations. There were, I think, strong and articulate reasons why the gay movement for decades refused to pursue the path on which it is now hellbent. They lay at the heart of an ethical vision of queer politics and centered on the need to resist the state regulation of sexuality. Queer thought both before and after Stonewall rested on these principles:

- It called attention to the mythology by which marriage is idealized.
- It recognized the diversity of sexual and intimate relations as worthy of respect and protection.
- Indeed, it cultivated unprecedented kinds of commonality, intimacy, and public life.
- It resisted any attempt to make the norms of straight culture into the standards by which queer life should be measured.
- It especially resisted the notion that the state should be allowed to accord legitimacy to some kinds of consensual sex but not others, or to confer respectability on some people's sexuality but not others.

- It insisted that much of what was taken to be morality, respectability, or decorum was, in practice, a way of regulating sexual pleasures and relations.
- It taught that any self-esteem worth having must not be purchased by a disavowal of sex; it must include esteem for one's sexual relations and pleasures, no matter how despised by others.
- It made itself alert to the invidiousness of any institution, like marriage, that is designed both to reward those inside it and to discipline those outside it: adulterers, prostitutes, divorcees, the promiscuous, single people, unwed parents, those below the age of consent—in short, all those who become, for the purposes of marriage law, queer.
- It insisted that any vision of sexual justice begin by considering the unrecognized dignity of these outcasts, the ways of living they represent, and the hierarchies of abjection that make them secondary, invisible, or deviant.
- It became alert on principle to the danger that those same hierarchies would continue to structure the thought of the gay and lesbian movement itself—whether through "internalized homophobia," in-group hostility, or simply through the perspective unconsciously embedded in so much of our thought and perception.
- It tried to correct for the tendency of U.S. debates to ignore other societies, on whom they nevertheless have an impact.

These insights and principles are so basic that they found expression equally in the work of academic theorists and untutored activists. They made up the ethical vision I encountered in the writings of 1970s gay activists when I was first coming out, and the same vision later served as the basis for much of the AIDS activist movement. Because of these basic commitments, when gay and lesbian organizations did include the expansion of marriage in their vision of change after Stonewall, they usually contextualized it as part of more sweeping changes designed to ensure that single people and nonstandard households, and not just same-sex couples, would benefit. In 1972, for example, the National Coalition of Gay Organizations called for the "repeal of all legislative provisions that restrict the sex or number of persons entering into a marriage unit and extension of legal benefits of marriage to all persons who cohabit regardless of sex or numbers." They also demanded "elimination of tax inequities victimizing single persons and same-sex couples." This may not have been a focused, detailed reform program, but it showed an insistence that the demands of couples be accompanied by those of the unmarried and of nonstandard households.

Those who now advocate gay marriage have not shown how doing so is consistent with this tradition. They have induced widespread amnesia about it. It is possible, at least in theory, to imagine a politics in which sex-neutral marriage is seen as a step toward the more fundamental goals of sexual justice: not just formal equality before the law, based on a procedural bar to discrimination, but a substantive justice that would target sexual domination, making possible a democratic cultivation of alternative sexualities. (This kind of question was explicitly ruled out of consideration by the *Baehr* court.) The advocates of gay marriage have not made this case. Many, indeed, have made the opposite case—that pursuing marriage means abandoning the historical principles of the queer movement as an antiquated "liberationism."

For writers such as Andrew Sullivan, Gabriel Rotello, Michelangelo Signorile, Jonathan Rauch, and Bruce Bawer, this is part of the appeal of marriage. Others argue, either ingenuously or disingenuously, that marriage has nothing to do with these historical commitments, that it is not a question of social change or cultural politics at all but a neutral matter on which each individual must decide. This is the official or semiofficial position of the major national gay and lesbian organizations: the National Gay and Lesbian Task Force, the Human Rights Campaign, and Lambda Legal Defense. Either way, the crucial founding insights behind several decades' worth of gay and lesbian politics are now being forgotten. If the campaign for marriage requires such a massive repudiation of queer culture's best insights on intimate relations, sex, and the politics of stigma, then the campaign is doing more harm than marriage could ever be worth.

For example, Robert Baird and Stuart Rosenbaum, editors of the reader *Same-Sex Marriage: The Moral and Legal Debate,* do not mention why the gay movement has historically refused to woo marriage. In their introduction, they try—briefly—to acknowledge some of the people who are so odd as to oppose it: "Among some gays, lesbians, and feminists, traditional marriage is integral to the corrupt authoritarian structures of society; it is a suspect institution embodying within itself the patriarchy they see as a cultural enemy of more desirable institutions." It appears from their strained, murky language that Baird and Rosenbaum cannot really imagine a gay argument against marriage. The sentence, which is supported only by a vague footnote to Monique Wittig as quoted by someone else, gets lost in obscure logic ("integral to," "embodying within itself"), indefinable nouns ("structures," "society," "patriarchy," and those "more desirable institutions"), and ponderous qualifiers ("*traditional* marriage," as opposed to marriage; "*corrupt* authoritarian struc-tures," as opposed to clean authoritarian structures; the "pa-triarchy *they* see"—poor things; a "*cultural* enemy," as opposed to a social or political or legal obstacle). This is a re-markably foggy description to be standing in for the most powerful tradition of thought on marriage to emerge from several decades of the queer movement. How did it come about that a book so uncomprehending could purport to rep-resent "the moral and legal debate"?

It is not unusual. Andrew Sullivan's *Same-Sex Marriage: Pro and Con,* manages little better. William Eskridge's *The Case for Same-Sex Marriage,* which shows at least a nodding acquain-tance with the history of gay and lesbian arguments against marriage, sidesteps the most telling arguments. Like Sullivan and Baird and Rosenbaum, for example, Eskridge deals almost exclusively with the brief article that Paula Ettelbrick pub-lished in 1989. But to Ettelbrick's straightforward claim that "marriage creates a two-tier system that allows the state to reg-ulate relationships," the best counterargument ventured by Es-kridge is that "to the extent that same-sex marriage might embolden some couples to be open, the institution might help all gay men, lesbians, and bisexuals." He then draws the con-clusion that "the greatest beneficiaries" of gay marriage would be "the next generations of homosexual youth," because they would have more open role models or, as Eskridge quaintly puts it, "a gay authority figure who can provide initial sup-port." (The paternalistic character of this argument is unmis-takable.) For queer youth, "the insider-outsider issue would seem almost irrelevant," Eskridge writes, despite the fact that all gay youth would be outsiders to gay marriage; that their minority would be a legally demarcated division between them and other queers precisely because of marriage; that age-of-consent laws, newly legitimized by gay marriage, would restrict not only their marrying but their right to other kinds of sexual relations; or that many of those youth, like queer adults, might aspire to a different kind of sexual maturity besides that of the married couple; and that such an alternative would be harder than ever to articulate or legitimate since marriage would have received the imprimatur of the very movement that had once come into being to open up different life horizons for them.

William Eskridge is no flake. Recently appointed to a senior position at the Yale Law School, he is the most prominent out gay voice at Yale, and perhaps the most widely respected authority on same-sex marriage. Yet, for the most part, he simply sets aside those arguments for sexual justice that would either reject or modify marriage. He accounts for their historical power by claiming that the leaders of the gay movement in the 1950s, 1960s, and 1970s were distracted by more pressing issues, or were themselves young, or were simply confused by the swinging ethos of the times. He thus gives himself permission to repudiate the social vision of queer politics. Worse, he does so in the name of AIDS, adding AIDS activism to his menu of forgetting:

> Whatever gravity gay life may have lacked in the disco seventies it acquired in the health crisis of the eighties. What it lost in youth and innocence it gained in dignity. Gay cruising and experimentation . . . gave way to a more lesbian-like interest in commitment. Since 1981 and probably earlier, gays were civilizing themselves. Part of our self-civilization has been an insistence on the right to marry. . . . The AIDS epidemic that ripped through the eighties not only cast a pall over the sexual freedom of the seventies but, more important, illustrated the value of interpersonal commit-

ment for gay people generally—and not just for safety's
sake. To the person with AIDS the value of a committed partner is incalculable. (58, 74)

Never mind that the "disco seventies" might have challenged Eskridge's prim notion of "gravity," or that they extended the sense of "dignity" to forms of life that he remains
willing to stigmatize. Never mind that the AIDS epidemic
hardly represented a loss of "innocence." Never mind that
many lesbians, far from standing as models of homey
monogamy, were at that time fighting the feminist sex wars,
or that many are even now developing a lesbian culture of ex-
perimentation. Never mind that many gay people have developed their own sense of what "civilizing" themselves means,
or that nonmarital sex and nonmarital intimacies have been
crucial parts of their alternatives. Never mind that it was homophobia, not AIDS, that "cast a pall over the sexual freedom
of the seventies," that it was precisely because of their viru-
lent hatred of gay sex that so many straight Americans neglected to do anything about AIDS and still continue to
impede its prevention. Never mind that "interpersonal commitment" can be a lousy prophylactic, if that's what Eskridge
means by "safety's sake." Never mind that it was precisely the
cultivation of nonstandard intimacies during the "disco seventies" that gave gay men the social networks with which to
support each other and rally in the midst of the crisis. Never
mind that the caretaking relationships developed by people
with AIDS have often differed dramatically from those that
would be legally recognized under Eskridge's reforms. Never
mind that from Eskridge's paragraphs on AIDS one would
never suspect that there was such a thing as AIDS activism, or
that it drew on the resources of the liberation movement to
elaborate a strong vision of health care and of a noninvidious

public recognition of diverse sexualities. AIDS, Eskridge almost seems to say, was a much-needed sobering lesson. It shut down gay liberation, and not a moment too soon.

This revisionist and powerfully homophobic narrative, taken over from the straight media, is indicative of the larger pattern in Eskridge's book in which the queer critique of sexual normalization and state regulation simply disappear. Everywhere in the current literature supporting gay marriage, one sees a similar will to ignorance substituting for engagement with the best of queer politics.

MARRIAGE WITHOUT COST

A much more benign position on marriage has become the creed of the major national gay organizations and is fast becoming entrenched as the new common sense. It is best expressed by Kerry Lobel, executive director of the National Gay and Lesbian Task Force, in a press release announcing support for gay marriage: "Marriage is an important personal choice and a basic human right. Whether gay people decide to get married or not, it should be our choice." This line of thinking was established by the late Tom Stoddard, who worked hard to launch both the gay marriage and military service campaigns. He wrote in *Out/Look* in 1989 that the fundamental issue "is not the desirability of marriage, but rather the desirability of the *right* to marry." Activists, in Stoddard's view, were obliged to work for as many options as possible for gay people, even if they disliked marriage in its currently sanctioned form.

A conception of activism as enlarging the life options of gay men and lesbians has a manifest appeal. And it is undeniable that many gays and lesbians want to marry. But this way of thinking says nothing about whether pursuing legal marriage is a good political strategy, about the ethical question of what marrying does, about state regulation, or about the normativity of marriage. Is marrying something you do privately, as a personal choice or as an expression of taste, with no consequences for those who do not marry? Is it a private act, a mere choice, like an expression of taste?

That would be true only if marriage were somehow thought to lack the very privileged relation to legitimacy that makes people desire it in the first place, or if the meaning of marriage could somehow be specified without reference to the state. As long as people marry, the state will continue to regulate the sexual lives of those who do not marry. It will continue to refuse to recognize our intimate relations—including cohabiting partnerships—as having the same rights or validity as a married couple. It will criminalize our consensual sex. It will stipulate at what age and in what kind of space we can have sex. It will send the police to harass sex workers and cruisers. It will restrict our access to sexually explicit materials. All this and more the state will justify because these sexual relations take place outside of marriage. In the modern era, marriage has become the central legitimating institution by which the state regulates and permeates people's most intimate lives; it is the zone of privacy outside of which sex is unprotected. In this context, to speak of marriage as merely one choice among others is at best naive. It might be more accurately called active mystification.

Evan Wolfson, making the same argument as Stoddard, quotes Arnie Kantrowitz as saying, "If it is freely chosen, a marriage license is as fine an option as sexual license. All I ask is the right to choose for myself, but that is exactly the right that society has never granted." Presenting marriage as an unconstrained individual option—a "license" in the same sense as "sexual license"—requires us to forget that it is a social sys-

tem of both permission and restriction. Kantrowitz's flip remark is more telling than he or Wolfson realizes, because he
has it exactly wrong. A marriage license is the opposite of sexual license. Sexual license is everything the state does not license, and therefore everything the state allows itself to
punish or regulate. The gay and lesbian movement was built
on a challenge to this regulatory system. But now we are told,
by the leaders of our own organizations in the United States,
that marriage is merely a matter of choice, a personal taste, a
right that some can exercise with no consequences, or with
only good consequences to others.

This line of thinking is reduced to its greatest absurdity by
the pro-marriage activist Mary Dunlap, who goes so far as to
argue that legal marriage will be necessary to preserve the
value of "diversity."

> The most important unresolved question about the
> value of diversity in this controversy is whether those
> of us engaged in the debate about lesbian and gay mar-
> riage can agree to disagree in our conclusions. If we
> can, then those who believe that lesbian and gay mar-
> riage can be a liberating and valuable step will be free
> to pursue it, while those unconvinced of its valuable
> potentials can pursue other avenues.

In effect, Dunlap's argument means this: Whoever gets
state support first wins. You are free to pursue "other avenues," but, of course, don't blame us if you find yourself
stigmatized, abjected, or criminalized. Just don't bother us
with talk about social justice for the unmarried, because that
would deprive married couples of their right to diversity.

The idea that marriage is simply a choice, a right that can
be exercised privately without cost to others, dazzles by its

simplicity. To most Americans it seems unthinkable that one might argue with it. And that is the key to its success, since it makes us forget the history of principled critique of marriage in queer politics. The same might be said of the other dominant argument for marriage: that it is just about love.

Many gay men and lesbians in America, echoing the language of Lobel, Stoddard, and Wolfson, seem to think that considerations of social consequence and institutional change are beside the point. They believe that marrying has nothing to do with the unmarried, nor with the state regulation of sex, nor with changing cultural norms. They seem to think that marriage is a long-term relationship of commitment between two people who love each other—end of story. "Whatever the history," Evan Wolfson writes, "today marriage is first and foremost about a loving union between two people who enter into a relationship of emotional and financial commitment and interdependence, two people who seek to make a public statement about their relationship, sanctioned by the state, the community at large, and, for some, their religious community."

This definition plays well to the kind of pious common sense that people nod along with as long as their everyday knowledge of sex and status is suspended. It is an exceedingly odd definition for Wolfson to offer in what is generally a tightly reasoned theoretical essay. A shrewd lawyer, he might be expected to know that love is not necessary for legally sanctioned marriage and vice versa. One can be married without love, just as one can love without marrying. Nor is the purpose of legal marriage "to make a public statement." You can make a public statement with any kind of ceremony, or by talking to people, or by circulating a queer zine. A legal marriage, on the other hand, might well be private or even secret. The *Baehr* court, which Wolfson celebrates, is more frank in its definition: "Marriage is a state-conferred legal partnership status." Wolfson mentions the sanction of the state only as a kind of amplifying power for the public statement of marriage, as though the state's role in marriage were nothing more. His definition works hard to mystify the institution. But it is typical of what passes for common sense.

Many gay men and lesbians who now say that they want marriage seem to focus on the way it confers, in their view, respectability and public acceptance. Often, they do not even mention the extensive slate of legally enforceable benefits, entitlements, and obligations that come with marriage. To them, marriage is a statement. For example, a writer named Barbara Cox asks: "How could a feminist, out, radical lesbian like myself get married a year ago last April?" (Of course it turns out that she has not gotten "married" in the legal sense; she means that she has had a private ceremony.) "My ceremony was an expression of the incredible love and respect that I have found with my partner. My ceremony came from a need to speak of that love and respect openly to those who participate in my world." In this way the state disappears when gay men and lesbians think about marriage. They assimilate it to the model of *coming out*. It is driven by expressive need. It speaks a self-validating truth, credible because it is "incredible." It is without invidious distinction or harmful consequence to others. It transforms the surrounding world, making what Cox calls a "radical claim." Even though people think that marriage gives them validation, legitimacy, and recognition, they somehow think that it does so without invalidating, delegitimating, or stigmatizing other relations, needs, and desires.

The naivete of this thinking is all the more striking because Cox writes as a legal theorist. Such is the world-canceling force of love that Cox can imagine the government as merely the most general audience for her private relations—another guest at the ceremony. Although she argues for legally sanctioned marriage, the transition from private ceremony to public regulation appears seamless to her. Ceremonies can do many laudable things, especially in making concrete the social worlds that queers make for themselves. They are a kind of public. But as a way of thinking about legal marriage, this notion of pure love, like so much else in contemporary U.S. politics, is an image of sentimental privacy. Love, it says, is beyond criticism and beyond the judgments of the law. Where law adjudicates conflict and competing claims, love speaks an inner truth, in a space where there is no conflict, no politics. It is the human heart, not ideology. Its intentions are pure. It has no unconscious.

I would argue that any politics based on such a sentimental rhetoric of privacy is not only a false idealization of love and coupling; it is an increasingly powerful way of distracting citizens from the real, conflicted, and unequal conditions governing their lives, and that it serves to reinforce the privilege of those who already find it easiest to imagine their lives as private. Then, too, the transcendent self-evidence of love leads people to think that any question of the ethical problems of marrying must be crass or at best secondary. If their unmarried friends ever express resentment about marital privilege, the married can always absolve themselves of their participation in marriage by appealing to the self-validating nature of their love—which strictly speaking should have rendered marriage unnecessary.

There is a further irony in the appeal to love as an argument for marriage. Love, as Cox describes it, is deeply anti-nomian—a revolt against law. Like Hester Prynne in Nathaniel Hawthorne's *The Scarlet Letter,* Barbara Cox is saying to her critics, "What we did had a consecration of its own." (Unlike

Hester, though, she thinks that it should therefore be conse-crated by law.) Love is self-validating. This claim for her love allows Cox to say that no one has a right to judge her and her lover. She directs this rebuke to gay critics of marriage, but it also extends to the fifty states, which, by sanctioning hetero-sexual marriage, are felt to pass judgments of illegitimacy on gay love. The appeal for legal marriage, in this way, is *also* a form of resistance to the legal character of marriage. That is why Cox can think of it as "radical," and why mass solem-nizations such as the one at the 1987 March on Washington do have at least some of the flavor of queer protests. Nothing shows the tensions and contradictions of our historical mo-ment more clearly than the way the upsurge of sentiment about marriage among gay people gives voice to an antino-mian protest—in the very act of demanding marriage.

In the antinomian tradition, love is more than a noble virtue among others, and more than a mass of disorderly and errant desire: it is a determinate negation of legality. Christo-pher Hill traces this idea back at least to the fifteenth century, when religious reformers known as the Lollards denied the necessity of church marriage. While the American Puritans concluded that marriage should be a purely secular matter left to magistrates, other reformers such as George Fox (whose followers came to be known as Quakers) questioned the validity of the institution outright: "The right joining in marriage is the work of the Lord only," he wrote, "and not the priest's or magistrate's for it is God's ordinance and not man's. . . . Friends marry none; it is the Lord's work, and we are but witnesses." After the Restoration, as government grew to be a more active participant in marriage, making marriage more and more a legal institution of the nation-state rather than a customary network of kinship, the appeal of love's rebellious-ness in the face of spreading regulation intensified. The legality of the modern state changed the background conditions of love.

In the early nineteenth century, the poet John Clare was able to describe an unsolemnized relationship as "Not felon-like law-bound, but wedded in desires." By 1852 the American physician M. Edgeworth Lazarus could write a treatise whose title says it all: *Love vs. Marriage*. In post-Romantic culture especially, the antinomian and world-canceling moment has even become necessary to validate love as love. That is why nearly all the great love stories have not been stories of marriages, but stories of extramarital or illegitimate love: Hester and Arthur, Tristan and Isolde, Catherine and Heathcliff, *The Bridges of Madison County, Titanic*. Occasionally a politics has been built on the basis of the antinomian strand. "We don't need no piece of paper from the city hall keeping us tied and true, no," sang the oft-married-and-divorced Joni Mitchell in 1971. But this politics has proven to be fragile, largely because it was built on the self-validating claims of the couple form, rather than on a recognition of other relations, intimacies, or sexualities.

After all, those stories of extramarital and illegitimate love may have prepared some people to do without that piece of paper from the city hall, but they have hardly brought the legal institution of marriage to an end. Most people who thrill to the spectacle of young, unwed lovers revolting against the horrors of an arranged marriage in *Titanic* do not imagine that marriage itself—arranged or not—might be dropped in the ocean as lightly as that diamond necklace. Why not? Why is the institution so resilient, even though so many have come to recognize that you can have a perfectly legitimate love without that piece of paper from the city hall? Is love any less valid because it has not been certified by the government? Most Americans would offer an instinctive and vigorous answer: no. Why does anyone imagine that love is an argument for marriage?

One reason may be that the couple form is sentimental-ized by the internalization of a witness—as when Cox speaks of her "incredible love"and "a need to speak of that love." One admires one's being in love. (As Robert Gluck writes in the opening sentence of *Jack the Modernist,* "You're not a lover till you blab about it.") Just as easily as the mass audience is per-mitted to sigh, weep, and throb during the lovers' most inti-mate moments, so also the state in its generality can embody the witnessing of that private consecration. When Wolfson speaks of making a "public statement," it does not seem sur-prising that the state is there, *sanctioning* it. One simply doesn't inquire into what it means for the state to sanction a statement. The state can piggyback on sentimentality in this way, making itself the silent partner and constitutive witness to what people imagine as their most private and authentic emotion.

The culture of marriage, in fact, thrives on stories of revolt against it. This has been true ever since the Enlightenment, when marriage ceased to be understood as an alliance of fam-ilies forged to preserve estates. The modern legal machinery of marriage is powered, paradoxically, by the love-couple's ability to transcend law. The state merely certifies a love that is beyond law; but by doing so, it justifies its existence as keeper of the law.

No other form of intimacy or sexuality has this power to couple with the state. One could make an antinomian claim to validity on behalf of, say, a blow job in a tearoom. Espe-cially if the blow job expressed a stigmatized, forbidden, and oppressed sexuality, the pleasure of its realization might be intensified by a sense of the wrongness of the law that banned it, as that law embodied an unjust social order and a lifetime of oppressive experience—all swept aside in the discovery, through pleasure, that the desire to reject that social order was shared with another. People in any nonnormative intimate or consensual sexual situation may in this way feel that they have turned the law under foot. It might seem in such moments that whether the emotion or the pleasure results in shared property or common respectability has no bearing on its authenticity. Outside the tearoom such claims would fall flat, lacking any reverberation in the carefully tuned wind chimes of sentimental couplehood. Whatever we value in a tearoom, or whatever we sentimentalize there, we don't sentimentalize it in a way that requires the state to be our solemn witness. The language of the love-couple is different. It wants recognition. It wants to rule.

Evan Wolfson draws on the powerful hidden resource of self-validating love when he argues that we have no right to question lesbians and gay men who want marriage. He believes that their desires must be valid just because they are desires:

> The suggestion that lesbians and gay men who want equal marriage rights do not know what is best for them as gay people is not uncommon in the intracommunity arguments against pursuing marriage. In the charge that the demand for equal marriage rights is insufficiently radical or liberationist, a contemnable [sic] desire to "mimic" or "emulate" the non-gay world, or a sell-out of less "assimilationist" or less "privileged" gay people, there is an inescapable whiff of imputed false consciousness. However, given the diversity and number of women and men within our communities who strongly want the equal right to marry, the imputation seems wrong, as well as unfair.

Wolfson is right, I think, to reject the idea that gays and lesbians who want to marry are simply imitating straights. That is a naive view of how norms work. He is also right to say that the argument against marriage has too often been put in these terms. But there is also a will to naivete in the implication that false consciousness cannot exist. What kind of reasoning would tell us that something could not be false consciousness because it was widely shared? Isn't that the idea? False consciousness is an undeniable force throughout history. From age to age, serfs have revered their masters, young men have marched gaily off to be slaughtered on behalf of deities and nations, and wives have lovingly obeyed patriarchal husbands. Why should gay people be immune to similar mistakes about their interests? It would not be surprising if they adhered to alien interests even on sober reflection. Marriage, after all, is a concrete personal benefit imbued with intense affect and nearly universal legitimacy. The alternative, a world capacious enough in its recognition of households to be free from such invidious regulatory institutions altogether, can easily seem abstract, even unimaginable. These options are not equally weighed, for the simple reason that marriage has a taken-for-grantedness and an apparently natural emotional force that prevent anything resembling rational choice.

Wolfson seems to assume that whatever passes as common sense must be right; people are never mistaken in numbers; their actions never have consequences that they themselves do not foresee; and they never act in a context the full ramifications of which remain unconscious to them. When he asks, rhetorically, "Does everyone who gets married, from Ruth Bader Ginsburg to Catherine [sic] MacKinnon, endorse every retrograde aspect of marriage?" he implies that the meaning of an act lies in the actor's motive. This assumption, characteristically American, obscures the issue. Whether an individual is right or wrong in choosing to marry, whether he or she is sincere or not, acting in false consciousness or not, or *intends* all of the consequences of marrying, has little to do with the ramifications of the act.

People might marry for all kinds of reasons. They might want to stick it in the face of the straights. They might want access to health care. They might want a public armature for their own will to sustain a relationship of care. They might have chosen with eyes wide open to embrace a world in which a coupling supported by shared property is the only sign of real belonging and the only publicly recognized context for intimacy. They might simply not trust the relationship to last without third-party assurances. They might think that marriage will relieve their fears of getting old, fat, or undesirable. They might marry for no better reason than that marrying is what one does. Or they might want in-laws. Judge Richard Posner worries, rather extravagantly, that a gay man would marry a succession of AIDS patients in order to collect the life insurance. It's likely enough that people will have many motives and that most will be marked by ambivalence. That's life.

Claudia Card illustrates well the difficulties posed by marriage for queers with nonstandard intimacies when she writes:

> My partner of the past decade is not a domestic partner. She and I form some kind of fairly common social unit which, so far as I know, remains nameless. Along with such namelessness goes a certain invisibility . . . We do not share a domicile (she has her house; I have mine). Nor do we form an economic unit (she pays her bills; I pay mine). Although we certainly have

fun together, our relationship is not based simply on fun. We share the sorts of mundane details of daily living that [Richard] Mohr finds constitutive of marriage (often in her house, often in mine). We know a whole lot about each other's lives that the neighbors and our other friends will never know. In times of trouble, we are each other's first line of defense, and in times of need, we are each other's main support. Still, we are not married. Nor do we yearn to marry. Yet if marrying became an option that would legitimate behavior otherwise illegitimate and make available to us social securities that will no doubt become even more important to us as we age, we and many others like us might be pushed into marriage. Marrying under such conditions is not a totally free choice.

This account reminds us that lived intimacies seldom take the form imposed by marriage. It also shows that people are likely to encounter in marriage a mix of constraints and that the meaning of marriage is only partly what they themselves bring to it.

Because the institution of marriage is itself one of the constraints on people's intimate lives, to judge the worthiness of the institution is not to condemn the people in it. But it does mean that marrying should be considered as an ethical problem. It is a public institution, not a private relation, and its meaning and consequences extend far beyond what a marrying couple could intend. The ethical meaning of marrying cannot be simplified to a question of pure motives, conscious choice, or transcendent love. Its ramifications reach as far as the legal force and cultural normativity of the institution. That is a heavy ethical burden to take on, and feminists such as Card have long shown courage in addressing it. No wonder people are so grateful to Wolfson, Lobel, and others who are willing to dismiss the ethics of marriage in such a radical and shallow way.

It is undeniable that the restriction of marriage to heterosexual couples is a potent form of discrimination, regulation, and stigma. But to combat that inequality requires us to think beyond the mere inclusion of gay couples and to recognize that marrying has consequences for the unmarried. Those consequences can be treated, roughly, under the following headings:

- the menu of privileges and prohibitions, incentives and disincentives, directly tied to marriage by the state;
- the material incentives and disincentives tied to marriage in civil society;
- the matrix of state regulations of sexuality of which marriage is the linchpin; and
- the broader cultural normativity of marital status.

Each of these should be challenged, not celebrated, as a condition of same-sex marriage.

The strategic question facing the lawyers is this: should we try to extend benefits and recognition even further beyond conventional marriage, uncoupling them from marital status and making them available to individuals, households, and intimate relations? Or should we claim for ourselves the status of marriage and thereby restrict entitlements and recognition to it? *This is not the decision that is posed to individual lesbians and gay men in the form of a choice to marry.* A poll of gay men or lesbians does not address this issue. We have good reason to be alarmed, given the potential for majoritarianism, when apologists such as Wolfson appeal to a silent majority that favors marriage. You need not argue that gays who marry have chosen to sell out less assimilationist or privileged queers in order to believe that the effect would be to reinforce the material privileges and cultural normativity of marriage. Individual choices to marry are not only rewarded with material benefits and normative recognition, but made from the limited slate of socially supported alternatives. Since the desire to marry is an aspect of the normativity of marriage, it cannot be said to validate the norm, any more than the desire to buy a Coke validates capitalism. Buying commodities sustains the culture of commodities whether the buyers like it or not. That is the power of a system. Just so, marrying consolidates and sustains the normativity of marriage. And it does so despite what may be the best intentions of those who marry.

Wolfson's view of marriage as simply a personal choice, like Cox's, or like Lobel's, is wholly inadequate to evaluate the strategy of pursuing legal marriage because it neglects marriage's legal and cultural consequences for others—those who resist marriage, as well as those who are drawn to it for a mix of reasons not of their own making. Whether they like it or not, married people have countless privileges, some that define marriage and some that ought to have nothing to do with it. They are taken more seriously than unmarried people; they are more likely to be invited to dinner parties, offered jobs, and elected to public office. In short, they have status. It is therefore hard to credit Wolfson's blunt assertion that the marriage issue is not about "the pros and cons of a way of life."

STIGMA AS SOCIAL POLICY

A more honest argument for gay marriage is made by those who know very well that to marry has consequences beyond oneself. Jonathan Rauch, for instance, has no truck with the illusion of choice or innocent diversity: "If marriage is to work," he writes, "it cannot be merely a 'lifestyle option.' It must be privileged. That is, it must be understood to be better, on average, than other ways of living. Not mandatory, not good where everything else is bad, but better: a general norm, rather than a personal taste." Similarly, Gabriel Rotello, in a cover story for *The Nation* excerpted from his book *Sexual Ecology*, argues that gay marriage would be a system of rewards and punishments designed to steer gay men into monogamy and away from sex with other partners. "Marriage would provide status to those who married and implicitly penalize those who did not," he writes. Rotello frames this argument in a behavioristic and economistic model that explicitly mimes the language of ecology: "In a culture where unrestrained multipartnerism has produced ecological catastrophe, precisely what it needed is a culture in which people feel socially supported as gay men to settle down with partners for significant periods of time."

I will leave aside Rotello's specious arguments about AIDS, such as his claim that it was "multipartnerism," not HIV, that "produced" catastrophe. I have elsewhere argued that his version of AIDS prevention targets public sex rather than HIV. Rotello at least acknowledges the normalizing intent of his argument about marriage. Most gay advocates of marriage, he notes, "are generally careful not to make the case for marriage, but simply for the *right* to marriage. This is undoubtedly good politics, since many if not most of the major gay and lesbian organizations that have signed on to the fight for same-sex marriage would instantly sign off at any suggestion that they were actually encouraging gay men and lesbians to marry."

Sullivan, Rauch, and Rotello hold contradictory beliefs: on one hand, all gay people are normal or want to be,

whether they know it or not, and pro-marriage politics therefore serves their interest; on the other hand, one of the principal arguments for gay marriage is that it would alter, indeed
normalize, the "behavior" and self-understanding of queers.
Again, Rauch is more honest than most:

> If gay marriage is recognized, single gay people
> over a certain age should not be surprised when they
> are disapproved or pitied. That is a vital part of what
> makes marriage work. It's stigma as social policy. . . .
> Heterosexual society would rightly feel betrayed if, af-
> ter legalization, homosexuals treated marriage as a mi-
> nority taste rather than as a core institution of life. It is
> not enough, I think, for gay people to say we want the
> right to marry. If we do not use it, shame on us.

Hardly anyone else has the guts to embrace the politics of
shame quite so openly in arguments for gay marriage. It is
generally implicit. William Eskridge at times pretends that
marriage is a noninvidious recognition of gay lives, but the
subtitle of his book, *From Sexual Liberty to Civilized Commitment,* reveals that it is rather a state-sanctioned program for
normalizing gay sexuality. (One reviewer noted that Eskridge's title bespeaks "the puritanical impulse to make bach-
elorhood equivalent to moral lassitude, where all sexual
expression outside wedlock is morally tainted.") When leading gay legal theorists dismiss gay sexuality as mere liberty,
uncivilized and uncommitted, it is no wonder that so many
gay men and lesbians feel either indifferent to or assaulted by
this campaign allegedly waged on their behalf.

Eskridge and others like him are not content to pass private moral judgment on unmarried queers. They see marriage
as an engine for social change and the state as the proper instrument of moral judgment. These deep assumptions about

the social welfare and the state's role are almost never challenged in the current debate. Even allegedly liberal writers,
such as the editors of the *New York Times,* typically endorse
the idea that the state's business is "to foster stable, long-
term" coupling. But this kind of social engineering is ques-
tionable. It brings the machinery of administration to bear on
the realm of pleasures and intimate relations, aiming to stifle
variety among ways of living. It authorizes the state to make
one form of life—*already normative*—even more privileged.
The state's administrative penetration into contemporary life
may have numbed us to the deep coerciveness in this way of
thinking. We take it for granted. Yet it is blind majoritarianism, armed not only with an impressive battery of prohibitions and punishments, but with an equally impressive
battery of economistic incentives and disincentives, all designed to manipulate not just the economic choices of the
populace, but people's substantive and normative vision of
the good life.

The ability to imagine and cultivate forms of the good life
that do not conform to the dominant pattern would seem to
be at least as fundamental as any putative "right to marry." If
so, then the role of the state should be to protect *against* the
abuses of majoritarianism. The claim that the state has an interest in fostering long-term coupling is profoundly antidemocratic. When the state imposes a majoritarian view of the
good life, it cannot claim to act on the basis of a neutral consideration of the possibilities; it acts to prevent such consideration. Andrew Sullivan, for one, makes the antidemocratic
impulse clear:

> There are very few social incentives of the kind
> conservatives like for homosexuals *not* to be depraved:
> there's little social or familial support, no institution to
> encourage fidelity or monogamy, precious little reli-

gious or moral outreach to guide homosexuals into more virtuous living. This is not to say that homosexuals are not responsible for their actions, merely that in a large part of homosexual subculture there is much a conservative would predict, when human beings are abandoned with extremely few social incentives for good or socially responsible behavior. But the proper conservative response to this is surely not to infer that this behavior is inevitable, or to use it as a reason to deter others from engaging in a responsible homosexual existence, if that is what they want; but rather to construct social institutions and guidelines to modify and change that behavior for the better.

Marriage, in short, would make for good gays—the kind who would not challenge the norms of straight culture, who would not flaunt sexuality, and who would not insist on living differently from ordinary folk. These behavioristic arguments for gay marriage are mostly aimed at modifying the sexual culture of gay men. Left and right, advocates of gay marriage assume that marriage as a social institution is, in the words of Bishop John Shelby Spong, "marked by integrity and caring and . . . filled with grace and beauty"; that it will modify "behavior"; and that a culture of "gay bars, pornography, and one-night stands" is desperately in need of virtue. ✓

This idealization of marriage is typical of those who are excluded from it: priests, gays, adolescents. It shows an extraordinarily willful blindness. As one observer notes: "to presume that morality follows on marriage is to ignore centuries of evidence that each is very much possible without the other." Worse, it is predicated on the homophobic equation of "gay bars, pornography, and one-night stands" with immorality—the very equation against which the gay movement came into being. If the conservative arguments *against* gay marriage reduce to almost nothing but homophobia, these arguments in favor of it are powered by homophobic assumptions as well.

It may be more precise to call these arguments anti-queer rather than homophobic, and as a way of commandeering the resources and agenda of gay politics, that's what they are. Yet the image of the Good Gay is never invoked without its shadow in mind—the Bad Queer, the kind who has sex, who talks about it, and who builds with other queers a way of life that ordinary folk do not understand or control. Marriage could hardly produce in reality the Good Gays who are pictured in this rhetoric: gays who marry will be as likely to divorce, cheat, and abuse each other as anyone else. The more likely effect is much uglier, since any politics that makes full social membership conditional on the proprieties of the marital form is ultimately a way to pave over the collective world that lesbians and gays have made. From the homophile movement until recently, gay activism understood itself as an attempt to stave off the pathologization of gay life—by the police, by the McCarthy inquest, by psychologists and psychiatrists, by politicians, by health and sanitation departments. Now we are faced with activists who see the normalization of queer life precisely as their role.

So it seems as though there are two ways to argue for gay marriage: embrace the politics of shame outright, allowing married gay couples to be relieved of stigma in order to make its coercive effects felt all the more by the unmarried; or simply deny that the legal institution of marriage has any connection to the politics of shame at all. It is of course possible, given the dissociative consciousness that prevails in American culture on the topic of sex, to believe both that marriage is a private choice without normative consequences *and* that it would make the queers behave themselves. It is equally possible, apparently, to believe both that marriage is just a neutral choice and that it is a crazy idea. ("Mad vow disease," Kate Clinton calls it.) Many gay activists who currently toe the party line—that marriage is simply a personal choice— privately oppose it. They feel uncomfortable publicly criticizing those who want to marry. Because no one is publicly voicing any opposition, the party line seems a safe way out. It also frees activists in the national identity organizations from having to recognize any connection between the gay marriage debates and the growing crackdown on all queerer forms of sexual culture in the United States. Apologists for gay marriage, such as Gabriel Rotello and Andrew Sullivan, can make that connection explicit again and again; yet the gay organizations have not entertained the possibility of such a connection long enough to take a stand against it. Too many activists see marriage only as a way of overcoming the stigma on identity and are willing to ignore—or even celebrate—the way it reinforces all of the other damaging hierarchies of shame around sex.

People who think that queer life consists of sex without intimacy are usually seeing only a tiny part of the picture, and seeing it through homophobic stereotype. The most fleeting sexual encounter is, in its way, intimate. And in the way many gay men and lesbians live, quite casual sexual relations can develop into powerful and enduring friendships. Friendships, in turn, can cross into sexual relations and back. Because gay social life is not as ritualized and institutionalized as straight life, each relation is an adventure in nearly uncharted territory—whether it is between two gay men, or two lesbians, or a gay man and a lesbian, or among three or more queers, or between gay men and the straight women whose commitment to queer culture brings them the punishment of the "fag hag" label. There are almost as many kinds of relationship as there are people in combination. Where there are patterns, we learn them from other queers, not from our parents or schools or the state. Between tricks and lovers and exes and friends and fuckbuddies and bar friends and bar friends' tricks and tricks' bar friends and gal pals and companions "in the life," queers have an astonishing range of intimacies. Most have no labels. Most receive no public recognition. Many of these relations are difficult because the rules have to be invented as we go along. Often desire and unease add to their intensity, and their unpredictability. They can be complex and bewildering, in a way that arouses fear among many gay people, and tremendous resistance and resentment from many straight people. Who among us would give them up?

Try standing at a party of queer friends and charting all the histories, sexual and nonsexual, among the people in the room. (In some circles this is a common party sport already.) You will realize that only a fine and rapidly shifting line separates sexual culture from many other relations of durability and care. The impoverished vocabulary of straight culture tells us that people should be either husbands and wives or (nonsexual) friends. Marriage marks that line. It is not the way many queers live. If there is such a thing as a gay way of life, it consists in these relations, a welter of intimacies outside the framework of professions and institutions and ordinary social obligations. Straight culture has much to learn from it, and in many ways has already begun to learn from it. Queers should be insisting on teaching these lessons. Instead, the marriage issue, as currently framed, seems to be a way of denying recognition to these relations, of streamlining queer relations into the much less troubling division of couples from friends.

WHAT IS MARRIAGE?

I have argued here that the *debate* over gay marriage has been regressive. Is that true of gay marriage necessarily? That depends in part on what kind of marriage we are talking about. The first thing to get over, in thinking about the possibility of a better politics and ethics of marriage, is the idea that marriage just is what it is. People mean very different things by marriage, and not simply because they are confused. If we begin by recognizing that it is a package rather than a single thing, it might be easier to imagine redefining it.

It is always tempting to believe that marrying is simply something that two people do. Marriage, however, is never a private contract between two persons. It always involves the recognition of a third party—and not just a voluntary or neutral recognition, but an *enforceable* recognition. We speak of entitlements when the third party is the state and of status when the third party is others, generally. Either way, marital benefits are vast.

Let us begin with the menu of privileges directly tied by the state to marriage. Marriage is nothing if not a program for privilege. "Marriage," as Richard Posner notes in *Sex and Reason,* "is a status rich in entitlements." The Supreme Court of Hawaii, in *Baehr v. Lewin,* handily lists some of those entitlements:

1. a variety of state income tax advantages, including deductions, credits, rates, exemptions, and estimates;
2. public assistance from and exemptions relating to the Department of Human Services;
3. control, division, acquisition, and disposition of community property;

4. rights relating to dower, curtesy, and inheritance;
5. rights to notice, protection, benefits, and inheritance under the Uniform Probate Code;
6. award of child custody and support payments in divorce proceedings;
7. the right to spousal support;
8. the right to enter into premarital agreements;
9. the right to change of name;
10. the right to file a nonsupport action;
11. post-divorce rights relating to support and property division;
12. the benefit of the spousal privilege and confidential marital communications;
13. the benefit of the exemption or real property from attachment or execution;
14. the right to bring a wrongful death action.

To these state entitlements would have to be added others, such as next-of-kin privileges in hospital visitation, medical decision making, and burial. There are also federal entitlements—including federal tax advantages or immigration and naturalization benefits—as well as local ones such as rent control benefits, already available to domestic partners in some cases. Even this list of state-guaranteed benefits, or rights, doesn't touch on the benefits that can be collected in civil society in the form of kin groups, discounts on and joint applications for services, memberships, and insurance policies—not to mention trousseaux, or the power to make all your friends and relations fly hundreds of miles to see you, wear expensive costumes, and buy you housewares from Bloomingdale's.

Most of these benefits could be extended to other kinds of households and intimate relations. Very few have a necessary relation to a couple or intimate pair—perhaps, logically enough, only those having to do with divorce. All the others could be thought of in different ways. Many, such as health care and tax equality, are social justice issues and should be extended to single people. Why should being in a couple be necessary for health benefits? Yet for many in the United States, it is. Health care is uppermost in the minds of many couples who apply for domestic partnership where it exists, and it is the issue that gives an edge of urgency to marriage. But think about the implication: that we happily leave single people uninsured. A just health care system would remove this distinctive privilege from marriage.

Other benefits, such as those having to do with property sharing, are specific to households rather than romantic couples and could be broadened to cover all cohabiting arrangements (ex-lovers, relatives, long-term intimate friends, etcetera). This is one of the most interesting features of PACS, the marriage reform proposed in France; it is a status giving legal recognition to living arrangements rather than regulating sex. It allows people to share property, inherit, and provide mutual care, whatever their emotional or sexual relation.

Still other benefits, such as immigration rights, parenting rights, rights to bring wrongful death actions, and even the prohibition against spousal testimony in court seem to be attached to powerful intimate commitments; but these need not be thought of as marriages. Such benefits could be extended to domestic partners, nondomestic partners of the kind described by Claudia Card, legal concubinage, or common-law relations. In Australia, for instance, immigration policy already treats all unmarried couples alike, whether gay or straight, under the "interdependency" category of the country's visa regulations. Even in the United States, a country not known for enlightened immigration policy, it was possible to win special consideration for intimate partners until 1996. Then Congress made it impossible for judges to waive deportation on humanitarian grounds, even in the case of partners who shared mortgages, businesses, or children. The painful separations that result from this policy testify vividly to the costs of marriage for those excluded from it. Gay marriage is not the only solution, nor necessarily the best one. Even if marriage were now allowed by a state, the Defense of Marriage Act prevents its extension to federal benefits such as immigration. It would be better if the right to intimate association were recognized and interdependencies valued in any form, not just the married couple.

Similarly, child custody could be linked to relations of care rather than to marriage. Gay and lesbian parenting arrangements very often involve three adults, rather than two, a situation that is denied by the attachment of parenting rights to marriage. Courts in some states have already made strides toward redefining family to reflect the reality of people's relationships. Why reverse that trend by linking everything to marriage?

The only kind of benefit that is necessarily linked to marriage is divorce. Even here, a number of different legal statuses could be made available to people, with different means of dissolution. This remains one of the principal differences between concubinage and marriage in French law, for example, and there is no reason why domestic partnership might not eventually be expanded so as to cover the same benefits as marriage, for both gay and straight couples, while allowing for less bureaucratically encumbered dissolutions.

Marriage, in other words, is defined partly by the bundling of various privileges and statuses as a single package. The argument for gay marriage no doubt appeals to many people because it is a shortcut to equalizing these practical social advantages. But the unmodulated demand for same-sex marriage fails to challenge the bundling of privileges that have no necessary connection to one another or to marriage. Indeed, if successful, the demand for same-sex marriage would leave that bundling further entrenched in law. Squeezing gay couples into the legal sorting machine would only confirm the relevance of spousal status and would leave unmarried queers looking more deviant before a legal system that could claim broader legitimacy.

Interestingly, the gay marriage debate almost never turns on specific benefits or entitlements. As the lawyer David Chambers notes, in the only extensive review of the legal entailments I have seen, "Whatever the context of the debate, most speakers are transfixed by the symbolism of legal recognition." Argument turns on the status conferred informally by marriage, on the function of marriage in altering "behavior," and on the real or imagined social purpose of marriage. This is an odd fact considering that the past several decades have seen many efforts to detach state entitlements such as spousal support from marital status, for straight and gay couples alike, and that these efforts have created new possibilities (for example, palimony). Extending benefits as an issue of justice, apart from marriage, reduces the element of privilege in marriage, as many conservatives fear. That strategy has enjoyed considerable success in the Scandinavian social democracies. The United States seems headed down the opposite path, given the revived popularity of marriage among straight couples and the generally conservative turn of the culture.

For example, the Family and Medical Leave Act of 1993 provides for leaves to care for spouses, children, and parents, but, as David Chambers points out, "makes no provision of any kind for friends, lovers, or unmarried partners." A Congressional commission on immigration policy, meanwhile, has widened the gap between the treatment of noncitizen spouses and the treatment of all other noncitizen relatives or partners. Republican reforms in the tax code are designed to provide further incentives to marry. Citing such developments, Chambers contends that gay couples will benefit from marriage. My argument here runs counter to Chambers's, but I find his evidence more useful to mine than to his own. Chambers shows that gay couples would gain many benefits from spousal status. No one doubts that. It does not follow that those benefits should be restricted to spouses, or that they should be bundled together, or that their acquisition by spouses would be either beneficial or neutral to unmarried queers. Chambers's review is admirably broad and detailed, but it does not show that same-sex marriage would be the appropriate solution to all the exclusions he documents. Rather, it shows, in case after case after case, that such areas of law as probate, custody, and immigration need far more sweeping reforms than same-sex marriage. Pursuing same-sex marriage as a strategy fails to address the privilege of spousal status that is the core of the problem. The conservative trend of shoring up this privilege is mirrored, wittingly or unwittingly, by the decision of U.S. advocates of gay marriage to subordinate an entire bundle of entitlements to the status of marriage.

Apart from the question of what benefits exactly we mean by "marriage," there is the more fundamental question about what the state's role in marriage is or should be. Government now plays a much more direct role in marriage than it has for most of Western civilization's history. In the anthropological literature, the main debate about marriage is whether its primary function in nonmodern society is to establish alliances between men, or lines of descent. In modern societies, marriage has less and less to do with either of these aspects of kinship systems. The powerful dynamic tension in premodern societies between marriage and the moiety system—in which your spouse is socially foreign to you, a representative of all that is opposite to your own kin—is lost and, for most moderns, unimaginable. In-laws are less and less material. Bastardy laws, where they remain on the books, seldom have an effect. People reckon family and descent through households, affinity, and blood rather than through the symbolic exchanges of ritual marriage. Some early modern features of marriage, like "publishing the banns," have all but vanished. Others, like the fertility ritual of flinging rice, survive only in vestigial form. Still others, like giving away the bride, probably retain more significance than anyone would like to admit. As these world-orienting horizons of kinship and exogamy systems have receded, the state as mediator has loomed up in their place.

In the contemporary United States, unlike most times and places in world history, state certification is a constitutive event, not a secondary acknowledgment of a previously established relationship. Some people naively imagine that marriage licenses are essential to marriage. But the marriage license is a modern invention. (Its history, as far as I know, remains unwritten.) Even the widespread use of parish registers to formalize marriages does not go back much before the eighteenth century. Until then, common-law marriage was the rule, not the exception. (In America it is currently recognized, even for heterosexual couples, in only one-fourth of the states.) Gay philospher Richard Mohr points to the importance of this fact, arguing that the best model for the legitimation of same-sex households would be common-law marriage.

In a common-law arrangement, the marriage is at some point, as the need arises, culturally and legally acknowledged in retrospect as having existed all along. It is important to remember that as matter of law, the standard requirement of living together seven years is entirely evidentiary and not at all constitutive of the relation as a marriage. . . . Indeed, that immigration fraud through marriage licenses is even conceptually possible is a tacit recognition that marriage *simpliciter* is marriage as a lived arrangement, while legally certified marriage is and should be viewed as epiphenomenal or derivative—and not vice versa.

To Mohr, this is an argument for common-law marriage. In my view, common-law marriage still suffers from many of the same limitations that other kinds of marriage do. But the distinction Mohr makes here is important, because it dramatizes how the state's constitutive role is simply taken for granted when we ask only whether we want "marriage." Countless systems of marriage have had nothing to do with a state fetish or with the regulatory force of law. Most of the options are not open to us. Others, more or less live, might be open if we did not think that the question was simply same-sex marriage, pro or con.

In a way, the common-law tradition seems to be what writers like Cox and Wolfson have in mind when they treat the state as if it merely recognized a marital relationship that the partners had created by themselves. This tradition harks back to a time not only before parish registers and marriage licenses, but before vice cops, income taxes, Social Security, and the rest of what we now call "the state." If American culture were better at recognizing what Mohr calls "marriage as a form of living and repository of norms independent of law," and if state recognition were more widely understood as deriving from that form of living rather than as authorizing it, then it might be easier to push the state to recognize single parents and other nonstandard households, interdependencies, and intimacies that do not take the form of shared property. In fact, all of these arrangements have gained status during the twentieth century. In respect to the family, real estate, and employment, for example, the state has taken many small steps toward recognizing households and relationships that it once did not. The current drive for gay marriage appeals to gay people partly because of that trend. People conclude, reasonably, that the state should be forced to recognize same-sex households as well.

But the drive for gay marriage also threatens to reverse the trend, because it restores the constitutive role of state certification. Gay couples don't just want households, benefits, and recognition. They want marriage licenses. They want the stipulative language of law rewritten and then enforced. Certainly *Baehr* has triggered a trend toward a more active and constitutive role for statutory law in controlling the evolution of marital practice. This trend comes at a time when the state recognition of nonstandard households is being rolled back in the United States and is increasingly targeted by a neoconservative program of restricting divorce, punishing adultery, stigmatizing illegitimacy, and raising tax incentives for marriage. The campaign for marriage may be more in synchrony with that program than its advocates intend.

Despite the *Baehr* decision, there is no sign that the strategy of demanding the package currently defined as marriage is working. In fact, like the rest of the "mainstream" program of gay politics—so often justified in the name of pragmatic realism—it seems to lead backward. The reaction to it further codified the distinctness of spousal status and its bundling. In Hawaii, the *Baehr* decision has not resulted in marriage for anybody. It has resulted in a number of new homophobic initiatives, including the referendum that allowed the state legislature to codify the heterosexuality of marriage. It has also given rise to a politically brokered compromise whereby, in order to win moderate and liberal support for the referendum, the state passed a new domestic-partner bill. It is the most sweeping domestic-partner legislation in the country. It might therefore seem to be a progressive gain. But there is a catch to it, in addition to its having been a sop to buy off critics of marriage: domestic partnership under the new law is available only to those who are not allowed to marry. For heterosexuals, in other words, it eliminates an alternative to conventional marriage. There have been two results: a sharper commitment by the state to the privilege of spousal status and a sharper distinction among couples on the basis of sexual identity. The first result, in my view, has been wrongly embraced by gay advocates. The second is the unintended consequence of their efforts.

The legal system is not likely to produce a clear verdict of the kind that its champions imagine. Given the spectacular political reaction against the campaign for same-sex marriage in Hawaii and Alaska, the outcome has been a definitive, homophobic repudiation of gay marriage for some time. Should the gay organizations win similar battles in Vermont, California, and elsewhere, the future would likely hold a long and complex series of state-by-state struggles over federal policy, the "full faith and credit" clause of the Constitution, and other limitations on the meaning of marriage.

Is Marriage a Step in the Right Direction?

Perhaps these are temporary setbacks leading to the eventual victory for same-sex marriage. And perhaps some readers will object that marriage, with all its flaws, might itself be a step toward further progress. How can we decide what the future is likely to hold? Marriage takes place in different registers, cuts across contexts. And, as we have seen, it can even express protest against itself. Who, then, is to say what its ultimate significance will be? The question is a real one; the situation is one of profound historical dynamism. But we cannot take for granted that marriage will result in progress on the package of privileges, prohibitions, incentives, and regulations that marriage represents.

Apologists for marriage rely on two contradictory stories about its history. Many writers, such as Evan Wolfson and William Eskridge, tell both at once, apparently not noticing the contradiction. In the first version, nothing about marriage changes. It is a basic human right, even though the details of marriage law may be socially constructed. In the second, everything about marriage changes, and for the better. Marriage is shedding its patriarchal roots. Gay people can push it to be something more radically egalitarian. Apologists for marriage hold both a fluid view of institutions and an often unquestioned commitment to the inevitability of progress.

Eskridge writes that his critics "come close to essentializing marriage as an inherently regressive institution." Evan Wolfson, in a logical leap that few Americans can resist, writes that marriage is "socially constructed, and therefore transformable." This view places a high rating on conscious will. It shoulders aside social structure and the unconscious dimensions of history. Some things about marriage, of course, we can transform. Others are part of our very perceptions and desires. That is what it means to be socially constructed. Even when we think we are transforming something, we are not free from the history that socially constructs both marriage and us. To say that marriage is socially constructed tells us nothing about how transformable it is, or how regressive it is. So light are the constraints of an institution on an individual, for Wolfson, that he can draw an analogy between entering the institution of Harvard (which one might do despite certain aspects of Harvard) and entering the institution of marriage. The analogy would hold only if everyone were supposed to have been born in Harvard, if it took special legal procedures to get out of Harvard, if there were an explicit slate of legal and economic disincentives for not being at Harvard, if Harvard had for millennia defined everyone's place in the structures of gender and kinship, and if all sexual activity outside of Cambridge, Massachusetts, were criminalized. Meanwhile, so deep is Wolfson's belief in progress that he argues that the question of strategy or priority is not important; same-sex marriage will be followed by further beneficial change, and anyone disadvantaged in the short term by the expansion of marriage will nonetheless be included in the step it represents toward full equal rights. (Note that this end point presupposes the first version of the marriage story, in which it is simply a right.)

American optimism in progress, riding a wave of triumphalism about "the end of AIDS" and the arrival of gay characters on sitcoms, has been able to sweep aside all objections and, it would seem, all evidence. At a time when homophobic initiatives are gaining ground at local, state, and federal levels, when even the movement to repeal sodomy statutes has all but stalled, the assumption of inevitable progress toward equal rights for everyone should give us pause. The military service campaign has resulted in a *higher* rate of military discharges for homosexuality under the "Don't Ask, Don't Tell" policy. The marriage campaign resulted in the Defense of Marriage Act and, for the first time, the codification into state and federal law of the heterosexuality of marriage. Both the military policy and DOMA were signed by President Clinton. Both sanction homophobia as national policy. Both exemplify an overreaching confidence in progress that has led to results that, even in their own terms, are regressive. These are minor policy matters, barely significant compared to certain antidemocratic structural trends, like the global corporatization of media. Everywhere we turn, in the United States and abroad, regressive tendencies mingle with and often overshadow progress.

Changes at the institutional level of the state seem likely to take many directions. Some, like the trend toward a more constitutive role of government in defining marriage, have been long in developing, are not consciously reflected upon in the debate, and can hardly be stemmed by the voluntary "appropriation" of marriage by gay couples. Many of the changes seem to have a local dialectical necessity; others seem highly contingent on political processes; others on the relatively autonomous legal system. In none of these areas can we assume that change will be progressive for anyone but marrying couples, especially in the absence of any organized effort to make it so. This way of thinking about the institutional character of marriage is also a way of saying that the normative question of the debate—will marriage normalize queers, or will queers radicalize marriage?—is posed too narrowly. It assumes either that marriage must mean a single bundle of status and privilege or that merely inhabiting the bundle can alter its fundamental meaning. The definition of marriage, from the presupposition of the state's special role in it to the culture of romantic love—already includes so many layers of history, and so many norms, that gay marriage is not likely to alter it fundamentally, and any changes that it does bring may well be regressive.

Like "heterosexuality," marriage is a contradictory amalgamation of histories and contexts, including:

- a stone-age economic structure of household formation and the traffic in women;
- a pagan and Christian symbolic order for male domination;
- the central institution that justifies the state's power to restrict sex in all other contexts;
- a distinctively modern contractual relationship of individuals, certified by the state and other third parties but usually understood as a private relationship of equality and intimacy; and
- an ancient ritual vocabulary of recognition and status—one that has a nonstate performativity quite apart from issues of state regulation.

Of course, there are plenty of conservatives for whom marriage is assumed to be a rational institution endowed with the forethought of generations and the loftiest purposes of mankind. They would have us forget that it carries over from the Stone Age. Each era of human history has given marriage a new layer of meaning, but at no point has any society been able to deliberate freely whether it wanted to inaugurate and enforce something called marriage. Moral rationales for marriage have always been created after the fact.

Perhaps the very complexity of this history encourages people to take a nominalist or antinomian view of marriage. Should we throw our hands in the air, concluding that there is just no way to tell what the future holds? That, too, would be a mistake. Not everything changes at the same rate. Some aspects of marriage are more stable than most cultural attitudes, so much so that in anthropology marriage has often been seen—ideologically, in my view—as the originating mechanism of social structure. Legal change also has an institutional gravity that impedes further change. In the face of all these layers of history, it is facile to say that gay people should "appropriate" marriage, or create their own meaning for it. Several of these historical layers are manifestly conflicting; hence the difficulty of saying how the addition of married same-sex couples into the multimillennial jumble would play out. These different aspects of marriage also have different implications for queers.

So I have my doubts when legal scholar Cass Sunstein, for example, argues that gay marriage would redress gender inequality by "subverting" traditional marriage, making it no longer the heterosexual matrix of women's subordination. This view enjoys great popularity among lesbian and gay apologists for marriage, including Wolfson and Nan Hunter. And not without reason. Hunter is undoubtedly right to claim that same-sex marriage would further weaken the model of subordination that has typified marriage. If marriage were not necessarily heterosexual, people could more easily view it as equal partnership. This is to say only that same-sex marriage might improve things, if not for queers then (indirectly) for women married to men.

Most claims for the power of marriage to transform cultural norms are even less clear and often contradictory. Richard Mohr, for example, asserts that the entry of gay men into marriage would loosen the knot of monogamy associated with marital status. Gay men, he writes, know that sexual exclusiveness does not have a necessary relation to commitment or love. The evidence bears him out. David McWhirter and Andrew Mattison report that only seven of the 172 male couples they studied were totally monogamous, and none of the couples that stayed together for five years or more were. (Similarly, Claudia Card notes an underrecognized tradition among lesbians of having "more than one long-term intimate relationship during the same time period.") Would we expect the figures to be the same if those 172 couples were in state-sanctioned marriages, with their status aura, their shadow-theater of stigma, and their web of regulations regarding adultery, privacy, and divorce? As we have seen, such writers as Gabriel Rotello and Jonathan Rauch confidently predict the reverse: marriage, they think, would curtail gay men's sexual lives. It would certainly cloak their sex in the invisibility of the zone of privacy, since that is one of the most noticeable features of marriage in the cultural imagination. (It was not Bill Clinton's relations with Hillary that made his sex life the greatest national media spectacle of the 1990s.) It seems rather much to expect that gay people would transform the institution of marriage by simply marrying. Morris Kaplan, in his book *Sexual Justice,* understates the issue when he notes, "This argument is not easily evaluated in part because it requires complex historical judgments and predictions concerning the effects of legal and social innovation."

Outside the legal system, change will certainly be complex. For example, introducing the mere possibility of marriage would vastly broaden the meaning of gay couples' refusal to marry. In fact, it would make gays' rejection of marriage a more significant possibility than it is now, by making it a free act. Thus, it is indeed plausible to claim that the historical process makes it difficult to predict fully what the evolution of marriage will look like.

It probably is true, to an extent, that gay marriage—at least, gay marriage *ceremonies*—would have a cultural impact similar to that of coming out. *I'm gay! I do!* Many of the gay people who now say they want marriage, like Barbara Cox, seem to want an intensified and deindividuated form of coming out. This desire is powerful, unanticipated, and interesting, to say the least. Gay marriage ceremonies, like the one staged by the Reverend Troy Perry in 1970, or the more recent wedding of two undergraduates in the Princeton University chapel, are performances in relatively unknown territory. They call attention to the nonuniversality of the institution. They force reactions in settings where the scripts are not yet written. They turn banal privacy into public-sphere scenes. At the same time, taking part in them is safer than coming out. Coming out publicly exposes you as a being defined by desire. Marrying makes your desire private, names its object, locates it in an already formed partnership. Where coming out always implies some impropriety because it breaks the rules of what goes without saying and what should be tacit, marrying embraces propriety, promising not to say too much. And where coming out triggers an asymmetry between gay and straight people, since straight people cannot "come out" in any meaningful way as long as the world already presumes their heterosexuality, marrying affirms the same repertoire of acts and identities for straights and gays. It supplies a kind of reassurance underneath the agitational theater of the ceremony.

The recognition drama of marriage also induces a sort of amnesia about the state and the normative dimensions of marriage. Discussions of gay marriage fall into characteristically American patterns of misrecognition; for example, the meaning of marriage is not social or institutional at all, but one of private commitment of two loving people; marriage has neither normative nor regulatory consequences for the unmarried, and is uncoercive because it simply fulfills the right to marry as a free individual choice; marriage means whatever people want it to mean; and so on. Gay marriage ceremonies lend themselves to each of these fictions. One can easily imagine ceremonies with a difference—in which people might solemnize a committed household, ironize their property sharing, pledge care and inheritance without kinship, celebrate a whole circle of intimacies, or dramatize independence from state-regulated sexuality. A movement built around such ceremonies could be more worthwhile and more fun than the unreflective demand for state-sanctioned marriage. Indeed, some people already experiment in these ways. Why do they get no press?

If one wanted to develop such alternatives, one would need not only the ceremonies, but some reflection on them. The issue is, after all, not merely a theoretical question *about* marriage, as though the debate did not have its own normative implications. The public sphere in which the discussion takes place is one of the contexts that *define* marriage. Although marriage has layers of meaning that are relatively resistant to spin, it is worth noting that the subject of same-sex marriage is so thoroughly mediated by public-sphere discourse that few can think about the topic apart from some kind of narrative about long-term social change, usually on the national scale. Mere mention of "gay marriage" triggers a consciousness of national policy dispute. It is as though a pollster and a reporter were in your bedroom, asking you if you wanted a judge or a cop to join the party. And always the issue implies not just abstract debates, like this one, but a story, a "news angle." No discussion of the issue can occur without some idea of what would count as progress. To take a view on same-sex marriage, pro or con, is implicitly to imagine movement toward some future or other: Whither America? Whither faggotry? Here, too, it is difficult to assume that the trend is one of progress. Or rather, what seem to be prevailing are regressive narratives of progress.

Andrew Sullivan's is one of the clearest, and the following passage from an article in *The Advocate* deserves quotation at length:

In one sense you can look at the gay male fondness for anonymous promiscuity as a rejection of all that our society values and offers. And you will find no end of "queer" theorists who will rush in to politicize such pathologies. "There is no orgasm without ideology," as one of them once (hilariously) put it. And you will also find no end of post-Stonewall gay novelists and playwrights who persist in seeing these one-night stands as some kind of cultural innovation or political statement. But for the rest of us, it isn't hard to see this proclivity for quick and easy sex as in fact a desperate and failed search for some kind of intimacy, a pale intimation of a deeper longing that most of us inwardly aspire to and deserve. Maybe this too is a projection, but I think I detect around me among many gay men both an intense need and longing for intimacy and an equally intense reluctance to achieve it—a reluctance bred by both our wounded self-esteem as homosexuals and our general inculturation as men.

But the answer to this reluctance is surely not a facile celebration of our woundedness . . . [T]here are plenty of people—especially among a few activist elites—who prefer to chant mantras of decades gone by and pretend that somehow this is 1957 and straight America is initiating a Kulturkampf against sex in parks and that somehow this is the defining issue of our times. But this is nostalgia masquerading as politics. It is not a "sex panic," as they call it. It is a victim panic, a terror that with the abatement of AIDS we might have to face the future and that the future may contain opportunities that gay men and women have never previously envisaged, let alone grasped. It is a panic that the easy identity of victimhood might be slipping from our grasp and that maturity may be calling us to more difficult and challenging terrain.

It is not hard to see what that terrain is. It is marriage.

You have to love something about this way of writing. It's shallow, it's mean, sure, but its style breathes new and bitchy life into jesuitical pieties you thought you would never hear in public again. Those pieties are packaged here as progress. The story works, for many, because it is rooted in a developmental narrative. It makes the "we" of gay people into a big individual who experiences history as the phases of maturation, like acne. The decades leading to and following Stonewall were our adolescence. Now we are adult, and ready to marry.

This, of course, is bad history. It dismisses even the adulthood of activists who disagree with Sullivan now, as well as that of all those who preceded him. It is also bad psychology, since it relies on a normative view of development that even a slight acquaintance with Freud (or with children) might have challenged. Of course, it will be said, Sullivan's "we" is just a figure of speech. But the rhetoric goes a long way toward legitimating, without argument, Sullivan's repudiation of queer politics. And it does so by relying on the way marriage marks out the narrative of life. Adults who marry are not necessarily more mature than adults who do not; often enough the reverse is true. Yet marrying is deeply embedded in the cultural unconscious as a sign of majority attained. It makes people feel grown up. What an extraordinary power we grant the government over our innermost lives! Nothing but the customary story of the life course grounds Sullivan's claim that marriage represents progress.

As a media strategy, too, Sullivan's ad copy for marriage is hard to beat, because it imagines the world from the view-point of an unmarked mass-media public, with no connection to queer life. When Sullivan writes that promiscuity is "a rejection of all that our society values and offers," he expects his readers to forget not only that many of them have found important pleasures and intimacies in promiscuous sex but also that in doing so they weren't rejecting all of society—only a hostile and restrictive version of morality. The reward for this largesse of forgetting is the ability to think of oneself as "society."

That's just the beginning of the amnesia required here. When Sullivan asks us to believe that the "pathologies" of sex and queerness are politicized by queer theory, we must forget that this rhetoric of pathology was itself politicized by the gay movement, and long before academic queer theorists came on the scene. The gay movement came into being only when the assumption that "homosexuality" was pathological was suddenly resisted—by people who kept the idea but challenged its connotations. The same thing has happened with "queer." Sullivan thinks that "to respond to the taunt of 'queer' by simply embracing it" is mere relativism, or "a facile celebration of our woundedness." Shouldn't the same logic apply to the way an earlier generation embraced "homosexual"? Can Sullivan not see that "queer," like "homosexual," is a way to embrace the term precisely in order to reject the framework of pathology?

When gay people express a desire to build their own world or to transform the rest of the world, Sullivan interprets this desire as a pathology—one that we are now happily on the verge of surrendering now that our "maturity" is about to be made possible by marriage. Isn't it really a stretch to imagine that a gay man going to a sex club does so in a desperate and failed search for the kind of intimacy associated with marriage? Surely if that were the goal, he would go about it differently. Perhaps Sullivan thinks it necessary to view all gay men as retarded in this way because he cannot imagine that there might be *other kinds of intimacy that* gay men have come to value and that they know how to find them. Do they go to the wrong place because "wounded self-esteem" somehow keeps them from dating and sharing property? Here, again, Sullivan, assuming a public stance not exactly calculated to raise the self-esteem of gay men, pathologizes those who don't match his ideal image. Even if gay men did suffer "wounded self-esteem," then wouldn't the most likely result be not promiscuity—which can take a fair amount of courage and dignity in defying the stigma and abjection associated with it—but rather the compulsive idealization of love and the desperate need to have validation conferred on one's intimate life by state-certified marriage? If you need legal marriage to give you self-esteem, then you can be sure that you aren't getting it. You're getting a privilege conferred by another. The need for official validation, not to mention the conformity that official validation rewards, is the opposite of self-esteem.

(I will leave aside Sullivan's notion that sex panics could not have happened after 1957, perhaps not coincidentally the last time it was possible to speak of "noble and ennobling love" without sounding like a Sunday school teacher. But then Sullivan could not have anticipated the irony of publishing his essay, full of ridicule for the idea that sex panics are a defining issue of our time, smack in the middle of the Lewinsky affair.)

Sullivan, in short, leaves every reigning norm in American culture unchallenged, except those bearing on the minor issue of the extension of marriage. Any other dissatisfaction with the world as it is currently ordered he dismisses as utter relativism, or victim pathology, or the quixotic desire to do without norms altogether. So aside from their wanting marriage, gay people have in his view no relation to the world except their undifferentiated belonging to "society." "Society" is an imaginary object, a vacuous term for the mass, and of course there cannot really be any question of belonging to it or not. Try *not* belonging to society. Sullivan's utopia is not in any event a social one; the grail he elevates is the worldlessness of love. As Hannah Arendt puts it in *The Human Condition,* "Love, by its very nature, is unworldly, and it is for this reason rather than its rarity that it is not only apolitical but antipolitical, perhaps the most powerful of all antipolitical forces."

In the name of love, Sullivan would obliterate not just queer theory, with its conferences and articles—that goes without saying—but the world-making project of queer life. Notice how much else he would have us shun: drugs and parties; the "post-Stonewall gay novelists and playwrights"; "activist elites"; drugs and parties; "sex in parks," and, indeed, sex out of wedlock anywhere; and the "mantras of decades gone by" (I imagine he is thinking of mantras like "Fight AIDS, not sex!"). Instead, he appeals to the private sentiments of "the rest of us." Who's left? A potent constituency, to be sure. But with no politics, no public, no history of activism or resistance, no inclination to deviate from the norm, and no form of collective life distinct in any way from that of "society." What we have left to "affirm and celebrate" turns out to be *couples* and those who are "manfully struggling" (perhaps with a whiff of bondage here) to be in a couple. Marriage is the perfect issue for this dequeering agenda because it privatizes our imagination of belonging. Thus the imagination of belonging appears, for Sullivan, only in a rush of redundantly massed privations that one would dismiss as bad and unedited writing if it were not so revealing of a conceptual impasse: the "pale intimation of a deeper longing that most of us inwardly aspire to." Do we have this "intense need and longing for intimacy," or do we only intimate that we inwardly aspire to have a longing for it? Whatever it is, it seems to be inaccessibly inward, deeper than something, intimated, so much less public than our own desires that we can only secretly long to long for it. Yet it is in this impossibly pure intimacy that we are supposed to be integrated, at last, with "society."

Given such rhetoric, the marriage issue can be understood as a way to wed the gay movement to the organized bad faith of the mass-mediated public that is increasingly its home environment. Only in such a realm could integration into a mainstream be imagined as our ultimate goal; only in such a realm could an idealization of marriage as simply equality and intimacy fail to be seen as a rather corny platitude; only in such a realm could people be induced to dismiss the richly depersonalizing intimacies of queer sexual culture as "ways we have used to medicate and alleviate the stresses of our lives"; only in such a realm could we seriously entertain a narrative of gay people commonsensically embracing marriage en masse, in the temporality of the headline, in a giant pink surge toward Hawaii; only in such a realm could this lurch toward a national altar be presented, as it is in Sullivan's essay, as a celebratory response to the end of AIDS, which he thinks has somehow arrived in the absence of a cure or a vaccine, and at a point when the most fundamental lessons of AIDS activism have been forgotten.

The success of Sullivan's argument depends on its ability to make its readers forget, in short, that they belong to a counterpublic. This piece of voodoo can also be stated as a predictive theory: *when gay people give up the perverse notion that they are perverse, they will discover that they have been nor-mal all along.* "Marriage," he writes, "is not, whatever its ene-mies say, a means to tame or repress or coerce gay men and women. On the contrary. It is, in fact, the only political and cultural and spiritual institution that can truly liberate us from the shackles of marginalization and pathology." Pathol-ogy is our pathology. Normally, we would be normal.

Meanwhile, what of the queer theorists for whom Sullivan has such scorn? What does queer theory tell us about whether marriage might represent progress? Sadly, not much. In much of queer theory, a view of the normal that is apparently the op-posite of Sullivan's turns out to be entirely consistent with his prediction about the politics of marriage. That is because it tries to evaluate the politics of marriage without making what Morris Kaplan calls "historical judgments and predictions con-cerning the effects of legal and social innovation." That either side can exploit the vagueness of our vocabulary here—"trans-form," "subvert," "change," "appropriate"—suggests that our theory has begged many of the evaluative questions. Kaplan himself, in an ostensibly Foucaultian analysis, hears the queer objection against marriage only as a "worry that success on this front would result in the assimilation of a distinct lesbian and gay ethos and to [*sic*] the imitation of heterosexist mod-els." This worry, he replies, "overstates the extent to which such recognition deprives individuals of the capacity to shape and revise the institutions they voluntarily create." Again, we see a faith in the voluntary creative efforts of individuals that would seem to be about as far removed from Foucauldian thought as it could be. Marriage here is considered only as "recognition." Its effects are described only for the individuals who are in it, and they, though shaped by the institution and its culture, are seen as shaping and revising and voluntarily creating marriage.

In *The Psychic Life of Power*, the eminent feminist and queer theorist Judith Butler takes as her problem the way "forms of regulatory power are sustained in part through the formation of a subject." This approach might seem promising well for the kind of problem we have been following. What Butler is trying to do is to explain the possibilities of queerness, subversion, and resistance as enduring despite the force of norms. What's more, she sees this subversion as inevitable in the formation of "normal" subjects. If this argument were successful, it would add up to the strongest possible rebuttal to Sullivan. He sees gay people as intrinsically normal but deluded into pathological queerness by the leagued forces of immature theorists, wounded self-esteem, and the prohibition on marrying. Butler sees all people as intrinsically resistant to the normal, even though they are formed by the normalizing "demand to inhabit a coherent identity." For Sullivan, gay men and lesbians are "virtually normal." For Butler, all creatures straight and gay are virtually queer. For Sullivan, marriage brings about the perfect normalization that gay people have wanted all along. It is only a slight exaggeration to say that for Butler, people have all along resisted, just by having psyches and bodies, the norms that form them.

Some readers—but not Butler—have drawn the conclusion that the further imposition of any norm such as marriage offers undiminished potential for queerness and resistance.

Butler's theoretical analysis, for these readers, produces a weak optimism: subjection is "inadvertently enabling." In the case of marriage, a change in the meaning of marriage might come about through a revision of key terms, including "self-esteem" and "marriage"; I have tried to suggest how this might be done. It will not come about merely by marrying and thus instantiating the norms of marriage, nor by having an unconscious and a body. No theory that takes queerness as inevitable in principle, or normalization as impossible in principle, can be of much use in making the world-historical judgment of the politics of gay marriage. Perhaps the theory was not intended for that purpose. But if such theoretical arguments lull queer theorists into a false optimism about the ability of queers to change the meaning of marriage, then it will have failed the aspiration to resist normalization.

Beyond Gay Marriage

Where does this leave us? Not at the altar, to be sure. In the straight press, and often in the gay press, the marriage issue is presented as the final frontier in the antagonism between gays and straights. Most queer people I know, however, do not see it that way. The marriage issue, defined as "same-sex marriage, pro or con," seems to most of us a lose-lose proposition for queers. The most disturbing aspect of the debate, to my mind, is that its framing has created a widening gap in the United States between the national lesbian and gay movement and queers. In addition to the arguments I have made here against the strategy of pursuing legal marriage as it is, we face a serious issue that threatens only to get worse: the campaign for gay marriage is not so much a campaign for marriage as a campaign about the constituency and vocabulary of the gay and lesbian public. The normalizing interpretation of marriage is increasingly established as the self-understanding of the national gay public. Whether marriage is normalizing or not for the individuals who marry, the debate about marriage has done much to normalize the gay movement, and thus the context in which marriage becomes a meaningful option.

Apologists for marriage often say that it would give the

gay movement new power to demand further reforms. What they do not take into account, besides the deep and nearly inaccessible power of the institutions and norms of marriage, is the change that the campaign is likely to bring in the movement itself—as its enemies are repositioned, its battles redefined, its new leaders and spokespersons identified, and as millions of dollars of scarce resources are poured into fights that most of us would never have chosen. In fact, since the campaign is not likely to result in same-sex marriage, despite the claims of its triumphal prophets, the most significant dimension of the marriage struggle may turn out to be these internal effects. On this score, and this score alone, Andrew Sullivan can claim tremendous success.

What makes these conservative or crypto-conservative activists potentially very powerful, though, is that they are the only people who are actively setting the cultural spin on the meaning of gay marriage as a transformative step. They are likely to succeed more than they might otherwise because they have stepped into a spin vacuum. Their arguments are echoed from the editorials of the *New York Times* to the commonplace comments of gay people on the street. It is easy to see why. The historical dynamic of cultural change is so volatile that very little can be predicted with much certainty from structural factors, so to the casual observer the conservative narrative sounds plausible—especially since there has been no competing narrative in which we could imagine same-sex marriage as a step toward further change, to benefit queers who are not in marrying couples.

Officially, the gay organizations, as Gabriel Rotello points out, are simply silent on the consequences of marriage for the unmarried. They claim to be neutral on the normativity of marriage, pretending that extension of matrimony would be only benign, that single people simply need not worry about it, because marriage would not be part of any normative program for change. So the field of opinion and self-understanding remains entirely open for the narrative in which sexual-liberty-to-civilized-commitment is simply the meaning of marriage. Because the dogma of the gay organizations is hollow at best, and in bad faith at worst, it demands a more morally inflected narrative about the future, interpreting the direction of change. The gay organizations have made no effort to provide a rival narrative of what the long-term goals and trends are or should be. The conservative story has become a dominant paradigm both because it is what many people want to hear and because it is *all* they hear.

Like the marriage issue, the struggle over the meaning of the gay movement is more than a matter of spin. The gap between gay and queer understandings of the movement is growing, I think, because of the structural developments mentioned in chapter 2: the changed nature of the AIDS epidemic; the decline of direct-action activism; the 1992 election and the rise of Clintonian politics; the growing importance of big-money political campaigns; the resulting prominence of a fat-cat donor base; the growing centralization of gay politics by national organizations headquartered in Washington, D.C.; the rise of highly capitalized lifestyle magazines as the movement's principal public venues; the consequent rise of a politics of media celebrity; and the heavy neoliberal spin on the movement in straight press and gay media alike. Under these combined conditions, the prospects for dequeering the gay movement are, indeed, bright. If it will ever be possible to pursue marriage as something other than a strategy to normalize gay sexuality, it will first be necessary to redevelop a queer public and, at the very least, to put a different spin on the issue.

In the early 1990s, marriage was pushed to the foreground of the national scene in part because Andrew Sullivan and others realized its potential for realigning American gay politics under these new conditions. Gay organizations have by and large accepted the mainstreaming project and, in particular, the elevation of the marriage issue as the movement's leading goal. The burden now lies on the advocates of marriage, especially the national gay organizations, to explain what they intend to do about the invidious consequences—intended or unintended—of their policy.

Is it possible to have a politics in which marriage could be seen as one step to a larger goal, and in which its own discriminatory effects could be confronted rather than simply ignored? I can at least imagine a principled response to this challenge that would include ending the discriminatory ban on same-sex marriage. It could not be a program that said simply that marriage is a right, or a choice. It would have to say that marriage is a desirable goal only insofar as we can also extend health care, tax reform, rights of intimate association extending to immigration, recognition for joint parenting, and other entitlements currently yoked to marital status. It would have to say that marriage is desirable only insofar as we can eliminate adultery laws and other status-discriminatory reglations for sexuality. It might well also involve making available other statuses, such as expanded domestic partnership, concubinage, or something like PACS for property-sharing households, all available both to straight and gay people alike. Above all, a program for change should be accountable to the queer ethos, responsive to the lived arrangements of queer life, and articulated in queer publics.

In the meantime, the triumphalist narrative—according to which we have emerged from the long night of marginalization into the full glory of our rights, our acceptance, our integration, and our normalcy—goes almost unchallenged.

Queer theory cannot counteract this narrative by insisting that we are inevitably, permanently queer. To do so is to give up the struggle for the self-understanding not only of individual queers—who may be persuaded despite their best instincts and the evidence of their daily lives that their sense of world alienation is their private moral failing rather than a feature of dominant ideology—but also of the gay world's media and publics, which increasingly understand themselves as belonging to a market niche rather than to a counterpublic. Queer counterpublics still exist and have not lost their vitality. But they have become increasingly isolated, as their connection with the national organizations, magazines, and publics has eroded. What will matter more and more is the world-making activity of queer life that neither takes queerness to be inevitable nor understands itself from the false vantage of "society." Because love, privacy, and the couple form obscure this effort, even the most generous estimate of the politics of marriage puts new pressure on keeping the world-making project in view. And because sexual culture and nonnormative intimacies are so commonly the practices of this world making, any argument for gay marriage requires an intensified concern for what is thrown into its shadow.

CHAPTER FOUR

ZONING OUT SEX

"When you have police everything looks queer."
—*Jack Smith*

Along Christopher Street, you can tell immediately that something is wrong. In Harmony Video, for years one of the principal porn stores on New York's most legendary gay strip, they now display $3.95 videos of football teams, John Wayne movies, and music videos by the fundamentalist pop singer Amy Grant. Just up the block stands Christopher Street Books, the store that proudly bills itself as "New York's oldest gay establishment." In the front room it, too, sells bargain videos that seem to have been unloaded by a desperate wholesaler in Kansas: Bob Uecker's Wacky World of Sports, and Spanish-language children's cartoons. Whose idea of gay merchandise is this? In the back room where the peep show booths are, they are playing films of wrestling matches. A few customers still come in, mostly gay men over forty. They leave quickly.

These surreal scenes are among the effects of Mayor Rudy Giuliani's new zoning law limiting "adult establishments," which the city began to enforce in the summer of 1998 after a series of court stays and challenges. As this book goes to press, the court challenges are not over and won't be for a long time. The law has already allowed the city to padlock dozens of stores and clubs, including a gay bookstore. But the law's details contain many gray areas, and the resulting uncertainty and fear have a much wider, chilling effect than the closures. "We're just showing wrestling videos until some more rulings come down," says John Murphy, assistant manager of Christopher Street Books. So far, building inspectors have not threatened action against the store. But the new law forbids adult business within five hundred feet of churches, schools, or other adult businesses, and the store is within a block of all three. "We've been here since before Stonewall," one clerk told me, "and there have never been complaints. The school and the church have no problem with us. Only the mayor." His anger is unmistakable, but it comes out in the flat intonations of despair. "The gay community used to fight this sort of thing. But no one seems to care anymore. And our clients aren't going to stand up and fight the law. Giuliani knew that before he started all this. But I thought some of the gay groups would fight harder."

Meanwhile, the street seems unnaturally quiet for a summer weekend. Ordinarily, in decent weather, the sidewalks overflow on Christopher, from Sheridan Square (the site of Stonewall) down to the Hudson River. People come from all over the city to walk up and down or to hang out at the piers by the riverfront. It's a queer scene: many of those who come are young black gays and trannies, mixed in with some tourists and the aging residents of the neighborhood. "This whole strip is going to die," says Murphy. "What do people

come here for? Cruising. They cruise, then they get something to eat, then they go in for a drink, and the whole strip
makes money." The queer life of the street here has already
been eroded, before the zoning law went into effect, by real
estate development, by a rise in tourism, and most of all, by
new policing and development on the riverfront. "You can
hardly go down to the piers at all anymore," Murphy says.
"They have curfews, they have fences, they have cops, there
are undercovers everywhere." A few blocks down by the
river, between two auto repair garages, stands West World,
one of the few adult businesses still allowed under the new
law. There, too, business depends on the vitality of the
Christopher Street strip, and the assistant manager is un-
happy with the rezoning. "If you start taking out places, less
people are going to come," he told the *New York Blade.* "We'd
rather that they didn't close those other places." And he, too,
says he has been surprised by gay apathy: "I thought the gay
community was more politically connected than to just let
things go."

In the mainstream press, the crackdown has been ap-
plauded by left and right. A victory for "all decent New Yorkers," the *Daily News* called it. The *Times* agreed, calling
rezoning an effective way to serve the "worthy purpose of protecting communities from the adverse impact of sex-related
businesses." (The *Times* editorialized in favor of the Giuliani
plan on no fewer than seven occasions.) Many gay people as
well think there would be nothing wrong with the death of
Christopher Street. Neighborhoods change, times change.
There will be new places to go. The gay neighborhood, for example, has already moved to Chelsea. And why not? No need
to romanticize the West Village, or be nostalgic about it.

One problem with this view is that Chelsea has no non-
commercial public space to match the old piers at the end of

Christopher. Its strip along Eighth Avenue is wealthier, whiter, less hospitable to nonresidents. The trannies are not going to hang out at Banana Republic. And the disparity is only going to get worse. Developing the Eighth Avenue corridor from Chelsea to Times Square was the principal goal of rezoning.

Of course, there are other neighborhoods. Across town, for example, the old Jewish and Latino immigrant district on the Lower East Side is home to a mixed and queer scene, less pricey than nearby SoHo, but already touted as the emerging fashion zone. Along with several new bars and restaurants, a new sex-toy store for women, called Toys in Babeland, has just opened. There, too, the effects of the zoning law are felt. Toys in Babeland is the project of two lesbian entrepreneurs from Seattle, where the parent store has been thriving for years. Clare Cavanaugh, one of the owners, told me that they are watching court rulings with a wary eye. (Sex toys are among the gray areas of the law.) In Seattle, their store has a large glass display window, lending queer visibility to the street and the neighborhood. In New York, the display windows stay empty, with nothing but discreetly drawn curtains. From the street, it looks like a podiatrist's office.

In Seattle, the store features a large selection of lesbian porn. In New York, the owners feel too unsafe to stock any. "It makes me sad," says Cavanaugh. "Women come in and want it. It's part of our mission to allow women to explore different parts of their sexuality. And when a woman comes in and says, 'I'm having trouble getting turned on,' I want to offer her a video. But I can't. We're taking chances as it is."

Farther downtown, the strip club Angels used to have a lesbian night. It was the only lesbian strip club in New York and a place where even the "straight" nights featured lesbian or bisexual dancers as well as trannies. Its owner had been one of the most vocal opponents of the new law. When the court stay on the zoning law expired, Angels became a primary target for enforcement, one of the first in Manhattan to be padlocked.

Uptown, Times Square increasingly looks like a theme park for tourists. The few remaining gay bars in the neighborhood are being closed by the city. Cats, for example, was a neighborhood gay bar, and one of the very few that welcomed trannies. The police raided it at midnight one night, found a few clients with joints in their pockets, and closed the place. Other gay bars in the area have been closed by similar tactics. Only two gay bars remain, and both are conservative enough that, as one patron told the *Village Voice,* "you feel like you're in a gay bar trying to act straight."

All over New York, in fact, a pall hangs over the public life of queers. Much more is at stake here than the replacement of one neighborhood by another, or the temporary crackdowns of a Republican mayor. As in other U.S. cities, sex publics in New York that have been built up over several decades—by the gay movement, by AIDS activism, and by countercultures of many different kinds—are now endangered by a new politics of privatization. This new political alignment has strong support among gays and lesbians, and the conflicts now flashing up illuminate the growing rift between identity-based lesbian and gay politics and its queerer counterparts.

The new politics is proving difficult to resist. For one thing, it happens on so many levels that its coherence is not always apparent. Zoning, for example, is only the most visible local form of the conflict. Consider the following developments as they affect the public sexual culture in New York.

1) In 1995 the New York City Health Department began enforcing the State Health Code, which prohibits oral, anal,

or vaginal sex, with or without condoms, in any commercial space. In the name of the health code, the city began padlocking theaters, video stores, and sex clubs—many of which had promoted safer sex. Some were allowed to reopen under court orders that even further restricted safer, and not just unsafe, sex—in some cases banning solo or joint masturbation in theaters and even "exposed genitals." The manifest contradiction of banning masturbation in the name of AIDS prevention caused neither the city nor the courts nor the local press to have doubts about this policy. Other businesses central to New York's culture of safer sex were chilled out of business by the harassments and publicity of the enforcement campaign. New sex clubs have since opened to take their place, a fact that Gabriel Rotello points to as evidence that there has been no "sex panic" in New York. But these new sex clubs, though numerous, are private, unadvertised, and in almost every case disconnected from any safer sex outreach. Even in the more or less above-ground sex businesses, like the West Side Club—all of which remain under threat of enforcement or harassment, and are thus compelled to deny that oral or anal sex takes place on the premises—safer-sex materials are nearly invisible. In the gay bars of New York, almost without exception, the free condoms that used to sit in bowls on the bar are no longer available. The posters and pamphlets that were ubiquitous in the 1980s are nowhere to be seen. Coming to New York from Amsterdam, or Paris, or Sydney, one could not fail to notice the difference. Sex has gone undercover. The consequence seems to have been the nearly perfect obliteration of a visible culture of safer sex.

2) Since 1994 the piers along the Hudson River waterfront—a legendary meeting place for queers for decades, and

more recently for youth of color—have been closed down, fenced off, subjected to curfew, and heavily patrolled, often by private security forces under contract to the state. Large stretches of the waterfront have been developed for upper-middle-class residences and tourism. Below the gay piers especially, the area down to Battery Park City has been turned into a tidy model of respectability. The city contracts the management of much of this space to private agencies, and already residents have been vocal in their resentment of non-residents who come to use the parks. The waterfront redevelopment plan, a joint agreement between city and state, currently contains no commitment to gay space or even open-use space on the waterfront.

3) In 1997 the Anti-Violence Project in New York reported a dramatic upturn in arrests of gay men for cruising, often on public lewdness charges. More than sixty men were entrapped and arrested in one bathroom in the World Trade Center alone. Other arrests were made on the streets of the West Village and Chelsea. Men cruising or just nude sun-bathing in the Ramble (the traditionally gay area of Central Park) were led off in handcuffs. Men of color, in these cases as in so many others, reported rougher treatment by police and higher levels of prosecution in the courts. The arrests were made not just by the NYPD, but even more by the Metropolitan Transportation Authority, the Port Authority Police, and the Parks Service Police. Sex workers, including transvestite and transgendered sex workers on the West Side, have also been harassed.

When the group Sex Panic! sought to help the Anti-Violence Project publicize these problems, the response from the local gay paper was simple denial. The numbers, it was said, though higher than previous years, were still no cause for alarm. It has since become clear that the numbers were no fluke. In 1997 forty gay-bashings were reported to the police in the first eight months of the year; the same period in 1998 saw seventy-two gay-bashings. Even while violence rises, the police themselves have become more industrious in efforts to entrap and arrest gay men. In Los Angeles, intensified campaigns against gay bars, sex clubs, and cruising grounds were waged by a special task force, and the city has gone to such absurd extremes as to ban pedestrians from walking certain blocks more than once in a half-hour period. Other examples around the country have been documented by the web site cruisingforsex.com, which posts regular cop alerts and bashing updates in its "Heads Up" area. In the last two weeks of April 1998 alone, the report included examples of entrapment and harassment from Miami; Gainesville; Las Vegas; Columbus; Oklahoma City; Charlotte; Los Angeles; Fort Lauderdale; Norfolk; Montreal; Spokane; McComb, Mississippi; Frederick, Maryland; Wilton Manors, Florida; Pompano Beach, Florida; Pomona, California; Anderson, South Carolina; Havre de Grace, Maryland; Hallendale, Florida; Long Beach, California; Tupelo, Mississippi; Savannah, Tennessee; and Bakersfield, California. Full information on the extent of the sex panics of the late 1990s is not available, and for a simple reason: the gay organizations have not gathered it.

4) Public space in general has dwindled in the city. The Giuliani administration, like the Dinkins administration before it, has awarded large tax abatements and other development incentives for corporations, often on the condition that the companies build or maintain a "public" area. (The Giuliani administration granted a record $666.7 million in tax

abatements by 1998, many of them for moving nonsex business into Times Square.) The result in the vast majority of cases is a sterile or semicommercial area, closed to loiterers or the homeless, heavily patrolled, and inaccessible at night.

5) Bars, dance clubs, and other venues of nightlife have been closed and harassed, sometimes for drug violations or on technicalities of cabaret license violations. (Bars can and have been fined or closed in New York if people standing in the bar are dancing.) Many actions against these venues are taken in the name of "quality of life," usually on account of noise complaints. Even the legendary Stonewall Inn has been targeted, as the West Village becomes a more and more high-priced and heterosexual neighborhood. Some bars, such as Rounds, the principal gay hustler bar, were closed on such grounds even though neighbors were not complaining. The chill on New York's nightlife and youth culture has been noticed by everyone.

6) Finally, there is Mayor Giuliani's zoning amendment, passed by City Council in October 1995 by a 41 to 9 vote. The Zoning Text Amendment (N 950384 ZRY) has the following key provisions:

a) A new definition of adult businesses. The old definition is a business "customarily not open to the public because it excludes minors by reason of age." The new one is vaguer and broader. It specifies businesses in which a "substantial" portion of materials or performances have "an emphasis upon the depiction or description of 'specified sexual activities' or 'specified anatomical areas.'"

These areas include nudity but also such things as "erotic touching of the breast, genitals, or buttocks." Included in this definition of "adult" are book and video stores, eating and drinking establishments, theaters, and other businesses. A preamble defines "substantial" as 40 percent; but because that number is not in the text of the law itself, enforcement agents can broaden it. The Giuliani administration has announced its intention to close stores it considers "adult," regardless of the percentages. In many (but not all) of the court cases to date, it has succeeded.

b) Adult businesses are allowed only in certain zoning areas. Most of these turn out to be on the waterfront. Almost all are poor neighborhoods, low in political clout. Many critics have pointed out that the city's maps showing the areas reserved for adult businesses are misleading, as the majority of land listed as available is in fact unusable. It includes, for example, Kennedy Airport. The mayor's office added some new areas to offset this complaint, claiming that the additions expanded the legal areas by 40 percent. The new areas turn out to be subject to the same complaints: they include land occupied by large hotels, corporate headquarters, department stores such as Macy's, and even City Hall itself.

c) Even in these new reserved districts, adult businesses are not allowed within:

—500 feet of another adult establishment; and
—500 feet of a house of worship, school, or day

care center. (These are called "sensitive recep-
tors" in the jargon of zoning.)

d) Adult businesses are limited to one per lot and
limited in size to ten thousand square feet.

e) Signs on adult businesses are limited in size,
placement, and illumination.

Enforcement of the bill is entrusted to building inspectors. The provisions of the zoning bill can be boiled down to
three forms of isolation:

- from concentration to dispersal (the five-hundred-
feet rule keeps adult businesses from being close to
one another);
- from conspicuousness to discretion (the signage regulations of the new bill are stricter than existing regulations); and
- from residential sites to remote ones.

All three impulses share the desire to make sex less noticeable in the course of everyday urban life and more difficult to find for those who want sexual materials. In April
1998, the city revealed that it would extend the new regulations to newsstand vendors, regulating the amount of
pornography sold at kiosks. (At the same time, new restrictions and higher licensing fees were imposed on the kiosks.)

The bill faced a court challenge on First Amendment
grounds, brought by the New York Civil Liberties Union and
the Coalition for Free Expression, a group representing owners of some of the city's adult businesses. The court challenge
was made on two grounds, both widely recognized in the
context of First Amendment law: secondary effects and rea-

sonable access. In brief, because government is prohibited by the Constitution from regulating speech for its content per se, the zoning of adult businesses is justified on the basis of its "secondary effects"—falling property values, rising crime, etcetera. Those opposed to the bill argued that the city failed to show that adult businesses have these secondary effects. The city's own published research, they pointed out, in some cases shows the opposite. Where there does seem to be a correlation between sex businesses and crime rates or low property values, the city has failed to show that the correlation is causal. It may very well be, of course, that porn stores go to those areas because rent and interference are both low. It must certainly be the case, too, that the low property values and crime rates result from other factors, like the proximity to the Port Authority Bus Terminal at Eighth Avenue and 42nd Street, which draws porn stores because of the travelers. Despite the high scrutiny that should have been devoted to these factors to make sure that the city was not singling out porn stores because of their content—which, of course, everyone knows was exactly the case—the courts allowed the secondary effects argument to stand.

The other ground of the challenge, reasonable access, means that the city can only restrict adult businesses by zoning if the zoning plan continues to allow access to Constitutionally protected forms of speech. On this score the challenge would seem to be especially strong, as the percentage of New York City land available for adult businesses—especially when nonviable sites such as City Hall Park are subtracted—falls well below the percentage that has been recognized in court precedents as allowing "reasonable access." And since most of the available land is in industrial waterfront areas that are badly lit, unpopulated, and remote from public transportation, forcing consumers into such areas is a way of imposing hidden costs for access. But the courts upheld the zoning law. Judges were unwilling to regard the legal issues as serious.

The examples I have given thus far come from New York City, mostly under the administration of Mayor Giuliani. The most common reaction among queer New Yorkers is simply to blame Giuliani and wait, passively, for a better regime. This is surely short-sighted. I have noted that similar developments are taking place in other cities, from California to Michigan and Texas. Even within New York, the politics emerging in the areas I've listed is not always coordinated policy, and Mayor Giuliani's "quality of life" campaign is only partly responsible. Several city and state agencies converge in response to different pressures.

Most are not, in my judgment, driven primarily by homophobia. The closing of the waterfront, to take one example, involves agencies of both the city and the state, as well as a private security force, all acting in the name of a common vision of real estate development. The zoning issue was clearly driven by real estate interests, even more than by the petit-bourgeois moralism to which it gave such venomous expression. Consider that the *New York Times* editorialized seven times in favor of rezoning; the New York Times Corporation is a principal member of the Times Square Business Improvement District. It was the Times Square BID, even more than Mayor Giuliani's office, that spearheaded the rezoning effort. The Walt Disney Company insisted on eliminating the porn stores as a condition of its role in changing Times Square.

We are therefore confronted with a problem of political analysis. What lies behind this erosion of queer publics, since it seems local and uncoordinated and yet widespread and systematic?

One common thread is the increasingly aggressive demand of market capital, which in the United States and elsewhere has seriously eroded the ancient ideal of an active public, a commonwealth. There is nothing new about that conflict, and commerce alone can hardly be said to threaten sex publics. It isn't just "the market" that is chilling New York's queer life. We might say, though, that the destruction of sex publics results from the new lattitude given to market forces in the Clinton era and from the corporate populism that wants everything visibly normal. One of the hallmarks of 1990s politics is a tendency to see the state as responsible for ensuring the expansion of market capital, rather than for fostering a democratic public sphere. It is thought to be a servant of the market, rather than a check to the market. So we hear more about "public/private partnerships," and less about the rights of citizens who don't happen to be corporations. This understanding of the relations among state, market, and public has become, in the late 1990s at least, a new common sense, one that appears *as* common sense partly because it arises in so many contexts that it seems to transcend the particularities and interests of any single context.

The current conditions in New York vividly illustrate what happens when national and international forces push the expansion of a market at the expense of public space and public autonomy, while at the same time lesbian and gay organizations decide that privacy and normalization are their goals. Gay men and lesbians collectively are exceedingly ill equipped at the moment to recognize or resist the shifts in public culture. The media that organize the lesbian and gay public have changed, along with the rest of the culture; they are increasingly dominated by highly capitalized lifestyle magazines, which themselves have been drawn into close partnership with the mass entertainment industry through the increased visibility of some gay celebrities and the increased use of gay-themed plots in mass culture. At the same time, a shift in the nature and temporality of the AIDS crisis has dissolved the counterpublic activism and collective will of the AIDS movement, now in spectacular disarray. Gay journalists are repudiating the legacy of safer sex, depicting lesbians as sexless homebodies whom gay men should imitate and gay male sexual culture as a zone of irresponsibility, narcissism, and death. Gay marriage is understood by many to offer a postpolitical privacy now described as the only thing we ever wanted. In this context the lesbian and gay movement has feebly resisted the trends I have described. The erosion of public sexual culture, including its nonnormative intimacies, is too often cheered on by lesbian and gay advocates.

The health department campaign against public sex venues was not just cheered by gay advocates, but initiated by them, in an intense publicity and lobbying campaign led by a small group of gay journalists. In the dispute over the waterfront piers, Sal Silitti, a gay member of the Christopher Street Block Association, called for closing them down entirely, telling the *Village Voice* that they were responsible for "an influx of polluting revelers." Both *LGNY,* the local gay paper in New York, and the news editor of *The Advocate,* a national gay magazine, responded to reports of public lewdness arrests by saying that if men were caught with their pants down, it was their own problem. *LGNY* also wrote that bar and club closings were proper enforcement of the law, and not a gay issue. When the rezoning of sex businesses was most contested in 1995, the gay playwright Terence McNally could only comment, "I don't want to live next door to a porn shop." (Later, in 1998, he expressed shock and outrage when the Catholic League for Religious and Civil Rights, denouncing his own new play as obscene, nearly managed to prevent it from being staged.) In each case, these gay people give voice to the ambivalence of stigmatized identity, and in each case it leads them to repudiate sex. Large numbers of lesbians and gay men—just how large we can only guess—embrace a politics of privatization that offers them both property value and an affirmation of identity in a language of respectability and mainstream acceptance.

Much of this reaction is familiar from the era of the homophile movement and later gay organizing. What's new about the current politics is that it is understood as post liberationist, a mark of gains already won. The history of queer public activity is now repudiated on the theory that its purpose has been served, that the highest goals of gay men and lesbians are now marriage, military service, and the elaboration of a culture in which sex plays no more of a role than it is thought to play in mainstream culture. Privatization can sometimes be embraced explicitly, as in the rhetoric of Larry Kramer and Michelangelo Signorile, but more often it is tacit, as in the unmistakable decline of street activism throughout the 1990s.

The "post-gay" rhetoric, however, can also mislead us into thinking that times have changed more dramatically than they have. In many ways, the conflicts over public sexual culture have changed little since World War II. Consider the following radio commercial, aired in New York City on May 10, 1998:

> They're cruising for sex all over New York. Sexual deviants are roaming our local stores and malls [sound of children laughing comes in], places that you shop, with your children. Monday, Fox Five's undercover camera catches perverts in very lewd acts in very public places [sound of jail cell closing and a police siren].

Could you or your child be an innocent victim of. . . .
CRUISING FOR SEX? On the Fox Five Ten O'clock
News, Monday.

The Fox story was one of many such attempts to capitalize
on the publicity following the arrest of pop star George
Michael in early April 1998 on charges of public indecency in
a bathroom. Punitive journalism and police actions of this
kind can be documented in great detail for every part of the
United States, apparently undiminished since the McCarthy
era. At least twenty local news programs around the country
used the same gimmick during "sweeps" week in 1998, taking undercover cameras into gay cruising areas to arouse normal America's punitive instincts.

It would be a mistake to see this tactic as simple homophobia. It is not that different from a local New York news
story run in 1995 on gay sex clubs, in which the camera was
led on a lurid undercover tour, allegedly to expose unsafe
sex. (Neither the cameraman nor the reporter, Mike Taiby,
thought it relevant that they had witnessed no unsafe sex.)
Although the target, in these accounts, is sex between men,
what matters to these watchdogs is not homosexuality per se,
but public sex. They aim to exterminate a practice and the
culture surrounding it, rather than an identity.

That is one reason why the punitive campaigns meet so
little resistance, even in the late 1990s, from the lesbian and
gay organizations. As countless studies of the tearoom and
bathhouse cultures of sex have shown, many men who participate in public sex do not see it as an expression of political
identity. Many—a majority in some studies, though lately this
has been disputed—think of themselves as heterosexual.
Many are married. Even those who consider themselves gay

may be seeking in such venues a world less defined by identity and community than by the negation of identity through anonymous contact; they may be seeking something very different from "community" in a venue where men from very different worlds meet, often silently, for sex. Because the politics of resistance was early defined in the United States along identitarian lines, while many of the most policed sites have been those where sex happens, and not those associated with a distinct identity, the organized lesbian and gay movement has traditionally been reluctant to engage in a principled defense of sexual culture outside the home. Gay organizations such as the Human Rights Campaign have not been committed to challenging the regulation of sexual practice by the state and by public media. On occasion they have been worse than indifferent. Torie Osborn, former head of the National Gay and Lesbian Task Force, publicly lamented the fact that sex "dominates gay male—and now young lesbian—culture," arguing that sex "holds no promise for real change; it is consumeristic and ultimately hollow."

Even the National Lesbian and Gay Journalists Association, in one of the few protests by gay organizations against the Fox news story, felt it necessary to preface its news release with a disclaimer by Karen-Louise Boothe, NLGJA president: "NLGJA in no way condones illegal sexual activity in public places." Here is the argument against the Fox story as the NLGJA conceives it:

> "Public sex [Boothe continues] is as foreign to the lives of most gay people as it is to most straight people. Males who engage in this practice with other males are usually those whose fear of societal condemnation makes them afraid to frequent clubs and bars where they risk being identified." Boothe said such stereotyp-

ical stories rarely examine the societal pressures that push people to have anonymous sex. What's more, day-to-day coverage on these stations often fails to present an accurate portrait of gay people living healthy and productive lives.

Public sex, according to the NLGJA, is a temporary evil that will wither and fade when gay identity is made more freely available to all. "Healthy and productive" means without sex in any public space; it does not occur to Karen Boothe that dominant criteria for "healthy and productive lives" might be precisely the issue. She does not imagine that the kind of privatization she urges might be regarded by some as a real loss. She also does not consider that her yardstick of value is that of normalization. "Public sex is as foreign to the lives of most gay people as it is to most straight people," she says; but one might as well respond: so much the worse for most gay people and most straight people. The fact that public sex is not the statistical norm ought to have nothing to do with its value or its morality. (Sainthood, when it comes to that, is "foreign to the lives of most gay people.") Boothe succumbs to the hidden lure of the normal, the confusion between what "most" people do and what one ought to do. Though she was one of the few people to speak out against the homophobic press frenzy after the Michael arrest, she utterly fails to challenge the stigma against men who find each other outside the home. In this respect, little seems to have changed since 1950.

I do not mean to be singling out the NLGJA, as there is nothing exceptional about Boothe's comment. The press release articulates both the new common sense and the premises of identitarian organization. If your only tool is a hammer, the saying goes, every problem looks like a nail. The institutional framework of the lesbian and gay movement, predicated on identitarian thought, sees all sexual politics as requiring a more consolidated gay identity and a form of life more fully conforming to the institutions of privacy. Now that the movement is in a further retreat from its history of radicalism into a new form of post-liberationist privatization, it is not surprising that gay men and lesbians are often willing to repudiate their own sexual culture and its world-making venues. The result is catastrophic weakness.

In a 1995 letter to the Planning Commission, Ruth Messinger, then Borough President of Manhattan, called attention to the unequal impact of the law on gays and lesbians. When Messinger ran for mayor two years later, Giuliani decided that it was the point on which she was most vulnerable. Citing her letter, he kicked off his official 1997 campaign by mocking her stand against the law. He then featured this attack in his television ads as the centerpiece of his campaign. It was a dare rooted in shame. His strategy was based on a cynical calculation that New Yorkers would not support the city's tradition of openness and diversity, but more particularly that gay New Yorkers would not rally to protect sex businesses and that Messinger would be isolated by the resulting stigma. It worked. The Stonewall Democratic Club, a gay organization, held a press conference supporting Giuliani's rezoning, asserting that Messinger had been misled by the advice of Sex Panic! and other radical fringe elements who do not represent the views of the lesbian and gay "mainstream."

Fortunately, activists at some of the lesbian and gay groups did see the danger in rezoning. But their constituency never roused itself. Along with many others, I took part in a coalition of groups that decided to fight rezoning in the political process, even though it was clear that its ultimate fate would rest with the courts. One of the most troubling aspects of the issue was the erosion of public support for a diverse, publicly accessible sexual culture; without this erosion the bill would never have gained support, and its passage shows a desperate need for new kinds of organizing and awareness. The coalition against it included anticensorship groups such as the ACLU, Feminists for Free Expression, People for the American Way, the National Coalition Against Censorship. It also involved a number of gay and lesbian organizations, such as Lambda Legal Defense Fund, the Empire State Pride Agenda, and the AIDS Prevention Action League. These latter groups joined the anticensorship groups for a simple reason, and it was this argument that Messinger echoed in her 1995 letter: the impact of rezoning on businesses catering to gay men and lesbians, but especially to gay men and other men who have sex with men, will be devastating. All of the adult businesses on Christopher Street can be shut down (or converted to outlets for football videos) along with the principal venues where gay men meet for sex. None of these businesses have been targets of local complaints. Since the Stonewall Riots of 1969, queers have come to take for granted the availability of explicit sexual materials, theaters, and clubs. That is how we have learned to find one another, to construct a sense of a shared world, to carve out spaces of our own in a homophobic world, and, since 1983, to cultivate a collective ethos of safer sex. All of that is about to change. Now those who want sexual materials or men who want to meet other men for sex will have to travel to small, inaccessible, little-trafficked, badly lit areas, mostly on the waterfront, where heterosexual porn users will also be relocated, where risk of violence will consequently be higher and the sense of a collective world more tenuous. The nascent lesbian sexual culture is threatened as well, including the only video rental club catering to lesbians. The impact of the sexual purification of New York will fall unequally on those who already have fewest publicly accessible resources.

It's also ironic that those who invoke AIDS in order to prevent anyone from having sex in a commercial space should also be trying to eliminate a porn trade that enables home consumption. Peep shows, masturbation, and porn consumption are, above all, safe. Porn stores are among the leading vendors of condoms and lube. And anyone with experience in AIDS education will tell you that the most successful tool against AIDS is a public culture of safer sex. Where will anyone find such a culture after the porn theaters, the bathhouses, the sex clubs, and the book- and video stores have been closed? Does anyone who works in AIDS prevention think that it's a good idea to zone all public sexual culture down to the waterfront?

The Giuliani administration has already done much to undermine that public world in which men find each other safely for sex and share a commitment to risk reduction. The health department wants to drive all sex into the home, a policy that is inconsistent with what we know about HIV transmission and with the tradition of safer sex education. A campaign against public sex is an easy sell in the Clinton era. A campaign against unsafe sex is harder. And for some reason it seems to be difficult for many people to remember the difference. At the very moment when we most need an inventive and publicly responsible activism, we see one privatizing initiative after another. In the second era of AIDS, now that information has gotten out and the short-term responses have to be replaced with lifelong solutions, and now that we are facing individual and collective denial about that prospect, our public sexual culture has to be a resource, not a scapegoat. If we turn the shaping of that culture over to city officials and tabloid dailies, we will have failed the challenge and left countless men with even fewer resources to face a future that few of us have the stomach to imagine.

It has been very hard to mobilize even gay resistance to any of these measures, and the rhetorical requirements of organizing in this context entail some very difficult and very theoretical questions. Maybe only a minority among us are regular customers of sex businesses. Why should the others care? Are my arguments against the bill only going to protect gay male culture? Am I also committed to defending what is sold on Times Square, including the worst of heterosexual culture? Will our position be justified on First Amendment, civil liberties grounds or on more substantive arguments about the benefits of public sexual culture?

What's Public About Sex?

There is very little sense in this country that a public culture of sex might be something to value, something whose accessibility is to be protected. Even when people recognize the combined effect of privatization initiatives—and in New York the effect is widely acknowledged—they find it difficult to mount a principled defense of a public culture of sex. Instead, they fall back on free-speech arguments. Although valuable, those arguments do not explain why you would want an accessible sexual culture. As we saw in chapter 1, isolation and silence are among the most common conditions for the politics of sexual shame. Autonomy requires more than civil liberty; it requires the circulation and accessibility of sexual knowledge, along with the public elaboration of a social world that can make less alienated relations possible. A public sexual culture is not just a civil liberty—like the right to deny the Holocaust and march in Skokie—but a good

thing, and queer politics should make it a priority. This does not mean that I am arguing against privacy. Quite the contrary: the politics of privatization, in my view, destroys real privacy even as it erodes public activity.

To see how this could be so, it will be necessary to get over the common misconception that public and private are always opposites. There are so many competing definitions of public and private involved that it may be worth listing the main ones:

Public	Private
1. open to everyone	restricted to some
2. accessible for money	closed even to those who could pay
3. state related	nonstate, belonging to civil society
4. official	nonofficial
5. common	special or personal
6. national or popular	group, class, or locale
7. international or universal	particular or finite
8. in physical view of others	concealed
9. outside the home	domestic
10. circulated in print or electronic media	circulated orally or in manuscript
11. known widely	known to initiates
12. acknowledged and explicit	tacit and implicit

13. "The world itself, in so far as it is common to all of us and distinguished from our privately owned place in it" (as Arendt puts it in *The Human Condition*).

Matters are further complicated by several senses of private that have no corresponding sense of public, including:

14. related to the individual, especially to inwardness, subjective experience, and the incommunicable;
15. discretely comported, in the sense of the French pudeur—expressible in English only through its op posite, impudence; and
16. genital or sexual.

None of these definitions are simple oppositions, or "binaries." Because the contexts overlap, most things are private in one sense and public in another. Books can be published privately; a public theater can be a private enterprise; a private life can be discussed publicly, and so on. So it requires no stretch of the imagination to see that pornography, "public sex," cruising, sex work, and other elements in a publicly accessible sexual culture are public in some ways, but still intensely private in others. "Public sex" is public in the sense that it takes place outside the home, but it usually takes place in areas that have been chosen for their seclusion, and like all sex involves extremely intimate and private associations. Sex work is public in being accessible for cash, but still private in many of the same ways, as well as being a private trade. When people speak of "public sex," the crudeness of the term misleads us about what is at stake.

The very concept of public sexual culture looks anomalous because so many kinds of privacy are tied to sex. One learns in infancy where one's "privates" are. This elemental relation to one's own body becomes the basis for a whole series of orientations: impudence and shame, modesty and display, upper and nether, clean and unclean, modest and lewd, and so forth. These charged polarities, with their visceral and pretheoretical force, come into play so quickly that it is often difficult, even with quite educated people, to discuss "public sex" and mean simply sex in spaces other than the home, or sex in commercial venues. It sounds like matter out of place, and in a way that triggers disgust. (The ability of sex in public places to reach such a primordial threshold of disgust, at once arbitary and unshakable, may of course be for many people part of its psychic and social appeal.)

Americans are most familiar with arguments for sexual liberties on grounds such as rights to privacy. Until the Rehnquist era, the Supreme Court on such grounds steadily limited the powers of the state to regulate sexual practice. The high point in this trend was the 1965 Supreme Court decision in *Griswold v. Connecticut,* authored by Justice William O. Douglas. The decision, which struck down a state law preventing the purchase of birth control, recognized a "zone of privacy" within which the government could not interfere with matters such as birth control. Twenty years later, the Rehnquist court shifted the direction of the law. *Bowers v. Hardwick* attached a new premise to Douglas's "zone of privacy": it is the heterosexual bedroom that is protected, regardless of what practices are performed or how the law refers to them. That is, laws that appear to ban oral or anal sex anywhere, even between married partners at home, cannot be invalidated by appeal to *Griswold* if the appeal is made on behalf of anyone other than married couples. (The Georgia sodomy statute was just such a facially neutral law.) The "zone of privacy" was recognized not for intimate associations, or control over one's body, or for sexuality in general, but only for the domestic space of heterosexuals. The legal tradition, in other words, tends to protect sexual freedom by privatizing it, and now it also reserves privacy protections for those whose sexuality is already normative. The privilege of heterosexual matrimony does not even need to be named, since it is able to pass in law simply as "privacy." As I pointed out in the last chapter, the privatization of sex in marriage would not be eliminated by gay marriage alone; it would be reinforced. And this is hardly privacy at all in the sense that most people understand. If your zone of privacy requires the support of an elaborate network of state regulations, judicial rulings, and police powers, and if it is based on the prejudicial exclusion of others from the rights of association or bodily autonomy you take for granted, then your privacy is another name for the armed national sex public to which you so luckily belong.

Richard Mohr, in *Gays/Justice* (1988), challenges the reasoning in *Bowers* on the basis of a strong conception of privacy: he argues that sex is "inherently private" and should be protected as such no matter where it occurs. The cultural taboo against public sex, he argues, stems from the phenomenology of the sex act. Sexual experience, he says, always excludes the everyday world of social status and individual will; its special somatic states of arousal, its altered sense of personhood, and its intimate relations all combine to remove people from the common order. The taboo against public sex acknowledges that threat, cordoning sex off to subordinate and invisible places. The very strength of that taboo, moreover, contradicts the state's claim to regulate consensual sex: "Across the range of actions for which there is an *obligation* to privacy, that very obligation generates, in turn, a *right* to privacy." With an admirable consistency, Mohr defends the kinds of public sex common to gay male culture precisely on the grounds of their privacy:

> Many may find orgy rooms at bathhouses and back-rooms in bars not to be private. This view is wrong, for if the participants are all consenting to be there with each other for the possibility of sex polymorphic, then

they fulfill the proper criterion of the private in the realm of the sexual. If, as is the case, gay cruising zones of parks at night have as their habitués only gay cruisers, police cruisers, and queerbashers, then they too are private in the requisite sense; and, in the absence of complaints against specific individuals, arrests should not occur there for public lewdness.

Involvement in a consensual sex act, for Mohr, presupposes a commitment to privacy, excluding all parties that have not consented and have not been chosen for participation. Consent distinguishes sex in public spaces from exhibitionism. And in spaces such as bathhouses and cruising grounds in secluded park areas, the assumption of privacy is reasonably grounded and should be respected.

Thus, in the *Fox Five News* promo quoted earlier, one of the most fundamental falsehoods lies in the implication that "sexual deviants" cruising in bathrooms are seeking to annihilate both consent and the privacy it creates: they "are roaming our local stores and malls, places that you shop, with your children." In reality, it is the journalist himself who must transgress both consent and privacy: "Monday, *Fox Five's undercover camera catches perverts* in very lewd acts in very public places." The need to resort to an undercover camera contradicts the claim that these places are already "very public." It also contradicts the claim that "you or your child" could be an "innocent victim" of cruising, since it implicates you in the aggressional and voyeuristic project of "catching" those who have no desire to be caught and who share a reasonable presumption that they will not be spied on.

Mohr's argument illustrates the intermingling of different senses of public and private in sexual culture. I think he is right to point to a kind of privacy—even intimacy—in the gay male practice of public sex, one that is very different from the privatization I see as characteristic of the new public morality. I also think that Mohr's liberal arguments are somewhat one-sided in choosing to defend sex only on the basis of its consensual privacy. The practices of public sexual culture, including both cruising and pornography, involve not only a world-excluding privacy but also a world-making publicness. The *Fox News* report is designed to undermine both. It replaces one privacy with another, one public with another: it violates the privacy of cruising in order to privatize the sex taking place there; and it reduces a rich public culture to inarticulate "deviants," consolidating instead a normal public in which it can be taken for granted that "you" have children, are at home, and go to "public places" in order to shop. The bad faith of this mass public is evident in the fact that the "deviants" are not imagined to have a rival point of view. And if the NLGJA protest is any indication, it must be admitted that the rival point of view remains badly inarticulate within the official publics of journalism and politics.

Within the culture of public sex, of course, very different recognitions and a very different articulacy are possible. The sexual cultures of gay men and lesbians are, after all, *cultures* in ways that are often forgotten, especially when they are treated simply as a mass of deviants looking for hormonally driven release. They recognize themselves as cultures, with their own knowledges, places, practices, languages, and learned modes of feeling. The naive belief that sex is simply an inborn instinct still exerts its power, but most gay men and lesbians know that the sex they have was not innate nor entirely of their own making, but *learned*—learned by participating, in scenes of talk as well as of fucking. One learns both the elaborated codes of a subculture, with its rituals and typologies (top/bottom, butch/femme, and so on), but also simply the improvisational nature of unpredicted situations. As queers we do not always share the same tastes or practices, though often enough we learn new pleasures from others. What we do share is an ability to swap stories and learn from them, to enter new scenes not entirely of our own making, to know that in these contexts it is taken for granted that people are different, that one can surprise oneself, that one's task in the face of unpredicted variations is to recognize the dignity in each person's way of surviving and playing and creating, to recognize that dignity in this context need not be purchased at the high cost of conformity or self-amputation. Within this queer world we recognize, usually tacitly, that the norms of the dominant culture would quash the scene we're participating in. It is therefore best understood as a counterpublic. Its openness, accessibility, and unpredictability are all marks of its publicness.

A public sexual culture changes the nature of sex, much as a public intellectual culture changes the nature of thought. Sexual knowledges can be made cumulative. They circulate. The extreme instances of this are in the invention of new practices or pleasures, as Michel Foucault noticed when he remarked that, with fist-fucking, gay men had invented the first wholly new sexual act in thousands of years. Even apart from this example, lesbians and gay men with relatively modest tastes can still recognize that their own bodies have been remapped by participation in a queer sexual culture, that each touch, gesture, or sensation condenses lessons learned not only through one's own experience, but through the experience of others.

The dominant culture of privacy wants you to lie about this corporeal publicness. It wants you to pretend that your sexuality sprang from your nature alone and found expression solely with your mate, that sexual knowledges neither circulate among others nor accumulate over time in a way that is transmissible. The articulated sexuality of gay men and lesbians is a mode of existence that is simultaneously public—even in its bodily sensations—and extremely intimate. It is now in jeopardy even within the gay movement, as gay men and lesbians are more and more drawn to a moralizing that chimes in with homophobic stereotype, with a wizened utopianism that confuses our maturity with marriage to the law, and perhaps most insidiously of all, with the privatization of sex in the fantasy that mass-mediated belonging could ever substitute for the public world of a sexual culture.

When gay men or lesbians cruise, when they develop a love of strangers, they directly eroticize participation in the public world of their privacy. Contrary to myth, what one relishes in loving strangers is not mere anonymity, nor meaningless release. It is the pleasure of belonging to a sexual world, in which one's sexuality finds an answering resonance not just in one other, but in a world of others. Strangers have an ability to represent a world of others in a way that one sustained intimacy cannot, although of course these are not exclusive options in gay and lesbian culture. This pleasure, a direct cathexis of the publicness of sexual culture, is by and large unavailable in dominant culture, simply because heterosexual belonging is already mediated by nearly every institution of culture. Publicness can have liitle of the sense of accomplishment or world making so long as it is the expression of privilege and conformity, so long as its putative wildness is compromised by the banality of normal heterosexuality, or so long as its distinctively male way of occupying public space remains a way of dominating women. The resentment that even heterosexuals feel toward these conditions can often enough find expression in the demonization of the very queers to whom publicness might still mean something different.

The learned knowledges of queer culture do not find expression in conflicts over public sexual culture because of the hierarchies of shame and memory in official speech. The conflict focalized in the Fox report—and equally in the Giuliani zoning plan—is more than a conflict between the privacy of cruisers and the public discipline of the state and the media. It is a conflict between a dominant public and a counterpublic, hierarchized by shame and silence. It isn't just cruisers who lose. It's everyone who belongs to the queer worlds that get more and more opaque to the normalized public view.

Writing in the *Village Voice* in 1995, Mark Schoofs quotes council member Walter McCaffrey's saying that customers of sex shops won't mind going to the waterfront because they "will feel much more comfortable going to someplace where they won't be seen." Schoofs continues: "This kind of 'comfort' is exactly what the right wing seeks, because it is not comfort at all. It is shame, and that emotion renders a person cowed, docile, and easy to oppress." This is why we don't hear more opposition to the bill, even though the extraordinary economic success of the industry shows that the porn trade has a broad popular base. Queers will be especially apt to understand this phenomenon, since it is so closely related to the effect that is called the closet. Common mythology understands the closet as an individual's lie about him- or herself. Yet queers understand, at some level, that the closet was built around them, willy-nilly, by dominant assumptions about what goes without saying, what can be said without a breach of decorum, who shares the onus of disclosure, and who will bear the consequences of speech and silence—by all of what Erving Goffman, in *Stigma,* calls "the careful work of disattention." Speech is everywhere regulated unequally. This is experienced by lesbians and gay men as a private, individual problem of shame and closeting. But it is produced by the assumptions of everyday talk.

This effect in the rhetoric of shame is more than simply an

individual affect. It isolates contexts and publics from each other, dividing them by amnesias. The rhetoric of antiporn activism is full of terms like "sleaze," "filth," and "smut." These words, conceptually vacuous, do nothing to say *why* porn is bad. It is impossible to argue with them; their purpose is not to provide reasoned argument. Their purpose is to throw shame, to make a rival point of view seem unimaginable. This effect takes place in interactions between persons, where it is familiar enough, but also in the interaction between different contexts for speech—in the circulation of discourse. People in everyday life often have fairly frank and open ways of talking about sex; in some contexts, such as talk shows, that frankness runs to the extreme. In the context of zoning, that frankness gives way to an implausibly general air of innocence. In one public opinion survey conducted in 1990 by Penn and Schoen Associates, 84 percent of those polled said Americans "should have the absolute right to buy all magazines and books judged to be legal." Yet in the context of the zoning debate, we have learned that large numbers of people will forget that opinion, supporting instead even more restrictive and punitive measures than those proposed by Giuliani. They are susceptible to the language of shame, the scenario of the pure and vulnerable child, the fantasy of an undifferentiated community standard. Such devices serve to hierarchize the contexts of sexual knowledge. They ensure that an official speech always trumps the knowledges of sexual culture, helping to thwart any possibility of cumulative and transmissible knowledge.

People commonly think public sex is the special province of gay men, those oversexed monsters of the urban alleys and the highway restroom. The same people who think this may have happily watched the movie *Risky Business,* in which Tom Cruise and Rebecca De Mornay have sex on the subway. They may have laughed their fucking heads off in the episode of *The Simpsons* when Marge and Homer romp around nude in public looking to spice up their sex lives. They may have identified deeply with the title characters of the show *Dharma and Greg,* who spend an episode competing with a friend to see who can have the most flagrantly public sex. They may own all of Madonna's albums. Yet the same people may think that there could be no defense for gay men who find one another in out-of-the-way corners of parks.

One advantage to thinking about the closet effect this way is to see how it can persist even after individual identities are declared through coming out. Even people who are out will often go along with the rules of decorum, forgetting in any official context whatever they might have learned of the queer world. These tacit rules about what can be acknowledged or said in public are as much a closet as any, and a politics of identity will be inefficient in fighting it.

Interestingly, the Giuliani administration and other advocates of rezoning higher up in the political system did not speak the language of smut, filth, and shame. Giuliani did not condemn porn per se—at least not until his zoning plan received court approval. His arguments were limited to secondary effects and a rather vague but politically potent language about "quality of life." This discretion had a legal rationale: he did not want the law invalidated in courts as a restriction on the basis of content. After the First Amendment challenge to the law had been rejected by two courts, Giuliani shed that tact as though it were a hair shirt and bragged openly that his tactics had succeeded in defeating the free-speech liberals. He also began advocating a more open deployment of shame, as the *New York Times* reported on May 16, 1998:

> Mayor Rudolph Giuliani, who prides himself on having a solution for everything, did not hesitate Fri-

day when a caller to his radio show complained about X-rated video stores and topless bars in the caller's Queens neighborhood.

"You know, one of the things you might want to do, which is perfectly legal: you can take pictures of people going in there," Giuliani said. "It really does cut down on business."

The mayor, a former U.S. attorney, used his weekly call-in show on WABC-AM to give the caller, Don, a little free legal advice, pointing out that it is legal to take pictures of people on the street.

"You know who goes into those shops, right?" Giuliani asked. "You know the kind of people who'd go in there. They probably don't want other people to know that."

This was going a little far, even for the *Times*. (The sex-offender laws recently passed by many states, however, go much further in punitive applications of public shame.)

At another level, of course, the assumption of unanimity behind the phrase "quality of life" produces its own kind of shame. There is a circularity in this rhetoric, since it serves to reinforce the disrepute of adult businesses and therefore helps to bring about the depression of property value that it appears to lament. More important, the rhetoric of "quality of life" tries to isolate porn from political culture by pretending that there are no differences of value or opinion in it, that it therefore does not belong in the public sphere of critical exchange and opinion formation. When Giuliani speaks of quality of life, he never acknowledges that different people might want different qualities in their lives, let alone that access to porn might be one of them.

The zoning bill seeks to privatize sex in part through this

segregation of sexual matters from the public culture in which differences between people can be recognized. Like the other rightist initiatives I've mentioned, it rests in a fantasy that persons in their public capacities as citizens and historical actors are nonsexual; they are, as Lauren Berlant puts it, "dead citizens." Persons in their sexual capacities remain in the zone of privacy whose heterosexuality is legally mandated and whose isolation from public culture the zoning bill tries to preserve. These twin fantasies, of dead citizens and sexual subjects, require massive and complementary amnesias. Citizens must routinely forget everything they know about sex. And sexual subjects must routinely forget everything they know about public culture.

Pornography and adult businesses jeopardize the amnesias separating sex and public culture in large part because of their physical orientation toward an indefinite public; they are media of acknowledgment. Having been reared in the bosom of Jesus, I never, it happens, saw gay porn until I began graduate school. I had had sex with men for years on the side, but I didn't think I was gay. I thought I was just wicked. The first porn images I saw, in a magazine belonging to a friend, set me suddenly to think, "I could be gay." Why did those pictures trigger my recognition when years of sleeping with men somehow didn't? It's because the men in the pictures were not only doing what I wanted to do, they were doing it with a witness: the camera. Or rather, a world of witnesses, including the infrastructure for producing, distributing, selling, and consuming these texts. This whole world could be concretized in places like Christopher Street or Times Square, but also in the formal language of pornography. In order for the porn to exist, not only did some of its producers have to have gay sex, they and many others had to acknowledge that they were having it. What is traded in pornographic commerce is not just speech, privately consumed; it is publicly certifiable recognition. This is part of the meaning of every piece of porn, and what is difficult to communicate in the dominant culture is that the publicity of porn has profoundly different meanings for nonnormative sex practices. When it comes to resources of recognition, queers do not begin on a level playing field.

The implicit publicity of porn is what feels so scandalous about it. The potentially creative effect of that publicity is lost from view in those versions of antiporn feminism that describe pornography merely as objectification or violence. One of the things porn objectifies is acknowledgment. And it provides this acknowledgment not just for identities that are already organized and recognized as legitimate. Let's remember that partly because of the environment of shame and phobia, many users of porn find queer pornography in predominantly "straight" businesses. Many are people who have not come to think of themselves as gay, who would have no access to the gay world at all if they were required already to be uncloseted enough to enter gay commercial spaces. Others pursue pleasures that don't fit the gay-straight map, and the extraordinary diversity of the porn industry can be essential for them. Porn enables unpredicted forms of experience. For this reason it can be especially important for young queers or for those who do not live in a gay neighborhood. Right now there is someone on Christopher Street who was drawn there by a hunger for that kind of acknowledgment. Those of us who have already fought our way to an identity and a supportive environment may feel that we no longer need that material evidence. But we still depend on rising generations of queers having access to it.

If it were not for the hierarchies of sexual shame that we saw in chapter 1, it would be hard to understand why conservatives see this as an important issue. After all, heterosexuals, queers, people in couples, orgiasts, priests—all kinds of persons—use pornography. Adult businesses catering to gays are a tiny minority even in Manhattan; only one specializes in lesbian material. The vast majority of the adult commerce is for presumptively heterosexual consumers. And given the increasing dominance of this market by video intended for home consumption, much of it is consumed in the very heterosexual bedrooms to which conservatives would like to see sexual culture confined. Yet some kinds of users are more at risk from the higher economic costs, and even more so from the higher costs of shame and the consequent burden of having to live without resources of acknowledgment, information, and culture building.

By intervening to cut off discussion and elaboration of the qualities of life, the zoning bill actually contradicts one important theme in the conservative vision of the state: the zoning bill, ironically promoted by those who routinely denounce government intervention and celebrate the market economy known as the "private sector," authorizes not only a massive state restriction on commerce but also state support for a particular vision of the good life. The bill brings the resources of the state into play in order to cultivate one form of life—already normative—by making it easier of access and acknowledgment than rival forms of life, which are not less legal, only despised and made artificially difficult.

The assault on legitimate pornographic commerce is particularly ironic given the enormous changes in the porn trade since the last attempt at zoning it out of New York, in 1977. Since then, the VCR revolution has made videotapes the lion's share of the porn trade. Unlike peep shows and stripper clubs, of course, videotape rentals are commonly taken to another space: home. Much of the panic about porn is not about what happens on Times Square, but about what people are doing with their home entertainment centers, which are harder for conservatives to regulate. There is no political gain in attacking the home consumption of commercial video. But if the video can be identified with its urban circulation zone, then—with a large dose of hypocrisy and no small irony—regulating it can be presented as a way of protecting the home from urban squalor.

The intervention of the state to weaken public sexual culture probably would not be possible without this form of hypocrisy—an ideology of space that demonizes some of the essential functions of a city in order to idealize an impossibly purified privacy. What the Giuliani people hate most is the secondary effects of porn concentrated in a neighborhood. The first aim of the bill's five-hundred-feet rule is to disperse adult businesses. Few of the bill's opponents challenged this provision. Even Manhattan Borough President Ruth Messinger, in her very thoughtful and closely reasoned letter to the City Planning Commission against the bill, continued to support the principle of dispersion.

But for queers the concentration of adult businesses has been one of the best things about them. The gay bars on Christopher Street draw customers from people who come there because of its sex trade. The street is cruisier because of the sex shops. The boutiques that sell freedom rings and Don't Panic T-shirts do more business for the same reasons. Not all of the thousands who migrate or make pilgrimages to Christopher Street use the porn shops, but all benefit from the fact that some do. After a certain point, a quantitative change is a qualitative change. A critical mass develops. The street becomes queer. It develops a dense, publicly accessible sexual culture. It therefore becomes a base for nonporn businesses, like the Oscar Wilde Bookshop. And it becomes a political base from which to pressure politicians with a gay voting bloc. Lesbians and gay men continue to depend on this pattern in urban space, no matter how much the promise of private identity—secured through property, rights, and legitimate couplehood—might invite them to repudiate the worldmaking scene of sex.

Phone sex, the Internet, and sitcoms cannot take the place of this urban space and its often unrecognized practices of sexual citizenship. That is what has been urged by columnists in the gay lifestyle magazines, chiefly Michelangelo Signorile. In his *Life Outside,* a jeremiad driven by resentment toward the social network he ambiguously refers to both as "the party circuit" and as "gay culture," Signorile fuses that resentment with a common rhetoric of antiurbanism. Fortunately, he claims, two millennial trends can be identified: the "deghettoization" and "deurbanization" of gay life in America. These, of course, are pseudo-trends. Signorile offers no evidence to support his claim that either one is happening. He does quote a sociologist named Jerry Kramer to support his notion that gay life is moving to the suburbs; but even Kramer adds: "at least that's my perception. I would say it's hard to tell how much of it is actually a movement out, and how much of it is gays and lesbians who were living in the suburbs before and are just coming out now because they feel more protected." For the reasons I've given, however, the growth of a suburban or rural gay culture would not lessen the importance of an urban one. To make that argument plausible, Signorile must rely on the rhetorical force of the notion of a "gay ghetto."

This hoary bugaboo is time-honored but deeply confused. No matter what aesthetic objections one might have to the styles and sociability of a particular gay enclave, there has never been a gay ghetto in the United States. A ghetto is an urban district in which a minority is confined, either by law (as in the Italian-Jewish quarter from which the word derives its name) or by poverty and systemic market effects (as in the case of black American neighborhoods, which gives the term its current moral force). A neighborhood voluntarily created, freely entered and left, and constituted only by massive concentrations of capital and middle-class commerce can only be called a ghetto by those deaf to the echoes of history or blind to the rules of power. A district like Christopher Street, in fact, is neither a ghetto nor a neighborhood, in the usual sense of the terms. The local character of the neighborhood depends on the daily presence of thousands of nonresidents. Those who actually live in the West Village—at this point, increasingly straight—should not forget their debt to these mostly queer pilgrims. And we should not make the mistake of confusing the class of citizens with the class of property owners. Many of those who hang out on Christopher Street couldn't possibly afford to live there. Many are African American, gay, and young. Where are they being zoned off to?

One of the most disturbing fantasies in the zoning scheme is the idea that an urban locale is a community of shared interest based on residence and property. In *The Death and Life of Great American Cities* (1961) Jane Jacobs long ago noted that, "As a sentimental concept, 'neighborhood' is harmful to city planning." Yet the ideology of the neighborhood is politically unchallengeable in the current debate, which is dominated by a fantasy that people are sexual only at home, that the space relevant to sexual politics is the neighborhood. The zoning bill is an ideal instrument for protecting the heterosexual zone of privacy because its procedural politics (Uniform Land Use Review Procedure, or ULURP) are set up to guarantee the dominance of the rhetoric of neighborhood at every step. The first requirement after the submission of the proposal was the meeting of every community board in the city, followed by the borough boards. Only then did the City Planning Commission hold public hearings at which non-neighborhood organizations could testify. But they were almost certainly given much less weight, and in the public media the assumption remained that people have a right to control their neighborhoods.

Terence McNally, for example, seems not to have noticed that whether he wants to live next door to a porn shop is irrelevant to the question whether porn shops should be allowed next door by law. The antiporn stance known as Not In My Back Yard (NIMBY) somewhat fantastically asks us to suppose that we are considering only the narrow issue of porn in our back yard. How many people in Manhattan have back yards? And does anyone, anywhere, have a porn store in his back yard? How does it come to pass that the nature of commercial urban space can be so flagitiously misrecognized?

The sexual culture of New York City serves people around the world, even if only as the distant reference point of queer kids growing up in North Carolina or Idaho, who know that *somewhere* things are different. Residents should not dictate the uses of the urban space around them to the exclusion of other users of the city. To do so is to fail to recognize what a city is. Urban space is always a host space. The right to the city extends to those who use the city. It is not limited to property owners. With the zoning scheme New York, perhaps the world's greatest metropolis, is pretending to be a suburb—though indeed one might want to ask whether a suburb is or should be in fact what it is in the NIMBY ideology: a geography of shame.

In the hearings before the City Planning Commission, the objection was frequently made that New York's unique culture would be jeopardized by the bill. The commission's only response comes at the conclusion of its report: "Suggestions made during the public testimony that the uniqueness of New York City precludes providing New York City *residents and neighborhoods* with protection against the negative impacts of these establishments are a disservice *to the many neighborhoods and individuals* of New York City and ignore the very real harm tending to stem from adult establishments." Even in the act of rebutting the objection, the commission deepens its assumption that the right to the city extends only to residents and property owners, that propinquity of domicile alone gives citizens the right to a political voice on the issue.

A better model of urban space might be elaborated from Henry Lefebvre's *Le droit à la ville (The Right to the City),* where we read:

> The human being has the need to accumulate energies and to spend them, even waste them in play. He has a need to see, to hear, to touch, to taste and the need to gather these perceptions in a "world." To these anthropological needs which are socially elaborated (that is, sometimes separated, sometimes joined together, here compressed and there hypertrophied), can be added specific needs which are not satisfied by those commercial and cultural infrastructures which are somewhat parsimoniously taken into account by planners. This refers to the need for creative activity, for the *oeuvre* (not only of products and consumable material goods), of the need for information, symbolism, the imaginary and play. Through these specified needs lives and survives a fundamental desire of which play, sexuality, physical activities such as sport, creative activity, art and knowledge are particular expressions and *moments,* which can more or less overcome

the fragmentary division of tasks. Finally, the need of the city and urban life can only be freely expressed within a perspective which here attempts to become clearer and to open up the horizon. Would not specific urban needs be those of qualified places, places of simultaneity and encounters, places where exchange would not go through exchange value, commerce and profit? Would there not also be the need for a time for these encounters, these exchanges?

Lefebvre rightly recognizes that the organization of urban space into lived worlds is undertaken by the city's users—not its planners, builders, owners, or rulers. He also recognizes that the worldliness of the city is inseparable from the possibilities of waste, play, and sex—in other words, from its more or less queer appropriations, which must be freed to find their own articulation as a public horizon. What Lefebvre imagines is the opposite of the geography of shame currently being mapped for New York.

Queer politics has a profound stake in public space and the sexual cultures it enables, and that interest needs to be made clearer in the language of the hay and lesbian movement. In the culture of privatization, however, organizing a city's users on any footing other than identitarianism can be extremely difficult. How else will it be possible to bring into awareness the stake that the city's users—regardless of their identity—have in its queer space? How, especially as public sexual culture is either repudiated as the relic of a bygone liberationism or defended merely as the indifferent expression of a civil liberty? Against these trends, my aim has been to bring to articulacy the publicness of sex publics, in all their furtive ephemerality, as a substantive good. I want to inspire queers to be more articulate about the world they have already made, with all its variations from the norm, with its ethical under-standing of the importance of those variations, with its ethical refusal of shame or implicitly shaming standards of dignity, with its refusal of the tactful silences that preserve hetero priv-ilege, and with the full range of play and waste and public activity that goes into making a world.

CONCLUSION

THE POLITICS OF SHAME AND HIV PREVENTION

Perhaps because so much of sex lies at the limits of consciousness and will—because it is a kind of experience in which we are supposed to be most ourselves, while at the same time least in control of ourselves—curbing sex can seem alternately urgent and impossible. The temptation to solve this paradox at the expense of others has been a fundamental theme in this book. Again and again, we have seen that people want to put sex in its place, both for themselves and for others. And the consequence, as we have seen, is not only that they create contradictions for themselves, but also that they create damaging hierarchies of shame and elaborate mechanisms to enforce those hierarchies.

The basic impulse to control sex is neither inhuman nor unreasonable. It is, in fact, exactly a wish to make sex reasonable, to force it to obey the dictates of common sense, or propriety, or simply self-esteem. What if our reasonable and highly esteemed selves could win out in this struggle? If sex were really to be made into a rational endeavor, something that we would never have to be ashamed of, would we not find that it had lost the very power that makes us value it: the appeal that we call, in a word, sexiness? No wonder it is so tempting to control the sex of others instead.

Nothing better dramatizes this paradox and its potential for frustration than HIV prevention. What could be more reasonable than to limit sex when it carries mortal hazard? And yet this is easier said than done. To many people—good, right-thinking, commonsensical people—it seems simply incredible that others still contract HIV through sex. How could anyone be so foolish? Some, indeed, are driven to indignation at the thought. After so many years and so many deaths, they think, anyone who still takes a chance must be either idiotic or criminal or both. Taking chances in sex may have been innocent enough in the early '80s, when no one knew better. But now, surely, there's no excuse. People who think this way are unlikely to think of themselves as villains; they are only being sensible. They often imagine that anyone who would disagree must be simply beyond the pale of reason. Since their own aim is to prevent HIV infections, it would seem that anyone who disagrees must be arguing *for* the right to transmit HIV, or for mere sexual libertarianism. (I should know; I have been repeatedly slandered in just this way.) What other point of view could there be?

Men who seroconvert as a result of sex with other men endure tremendous shame because of this common attitude. They know that they will be blamed for contracting HIV through sex, no less now than in the early years of the epidemic, and possibly more because they will be blamed as irrational, or sexually addicted, and not just as homosexual. The shame of seroconversion is intensified because most men who get infected have the same attitude themselves. The evidence does not suggest that very many HIV infections result from people who simply have no fear of the virus, who take no precautions whatever, who have lost their reason, or who burn with suicidal rage against humanity, who actually *like* having the virus, or who think they have the right to transmit it. So why does the problem persist?

It cannot be denied that HIV continues to be contracted through sex, through unprotected sex in more than half of all new infections. The fastest growing group of people with HIV is women (for whom the increase in AIDS incidence since 1991 is an astonishing 70 percent), and especially women of color. Many have contracted HIV through heterosexual relations, in which the imbalance of power between men and women remains central and inadequately addressed as an issue of public health. Gay men of all races, however, continue to represent a disproportionate number of HIV and AIDS cases. Have they contracted HIV of their own free will? Are they to be regarded as fools? Wantons? Villains? What would it take to stop them?

From the beginning, AIDS has affected most those populations lowest in the hierarchy of respectability, and too often people have thought that the way to stop new infections was to stop people from having sex or using drugs, or to punish those who could not be made to stop. The Clinton administration still refuses to support needle-exchange programs, which have been proven to save lives, for fear of being labeled soft on drugs. Clinton's cynical calculation has been made easier by the general sense that AIDS is over, and indeed he no longer mentions AIDS in his annual state of the union address. As the epidemic becomes more racialized, and as a myth of universal progress takes hold among gay men, it has become easier and easier to treat the problem of risk merely through aversion. This attitude has become common even among those gay men who in earlier stages of the epidemic fought against the stigma of HIV.

AVERSION AS PUBLIC HEALTH

The dynamics of shame helps to explain continuing rates of infection on a number of levels: for individuals, shame and stigma give risk much of its appeal and make it hard for people to reflect on that risk; for public policy, the pseudo-morality of shame leads to counterproductive measures. The trend in public policy and opinion, in fact, has been away from support for the culture of safer sex, and toward more punitive approaches. Now, when new medical advances make it possible to curb the spread of HIV dramatically, the politics of stigma continues to distort prevention efforts, often disastrously. To say this is to buck common wisdom, since a very different story about the history of HIV prevention seems to prevail these days. It goes like this:

Back in the old days, children, bad men like Jesse Helms used to wave safe-sex comic books on the floor of the Senate, saying the homos made them sick. They used to pass laws to keep tax money away from safer sex programs. Thank Jesus those days are gone. First, we shut down the bathhouses. Then we got everyone to use condoms. Then Bill Clinton came into office, and he cares about AIDS. Then the new protease inhibitors came along, and they saved everyone's life. Now we do prevention right. There are still some bad men out there, having unsafe sex. But now we put the police on them. Yes indeed, HIV prevention sure has come a long way.

In fact, most of the progress that people take for granted is deceptive. Treatment for people with AIDS has dramatically improved for the tiny minority who have full health care.

That much is undeniable. But that very success has led to the conviction that AIDS is no longer the serious threat that it once was. The much-publicized decline in the AIDS-related deaths conceals a ballooning crisis in AIDS services, and especially in primary prevention. It is always easy to forget that 95 percent of people with HIV live in developing countries where AIDS-related deaths are rising rather than declining. In the developed nations, especially those with universal health care, the advent of protease inhibitors created an opportunity to stop the spread of HIV, because the new treatments somewhat reduced the infectivity of those who already had the virus. This opportunity has been squandered, at least in the United States. The American health care system (if it can be called a system) magnifies inequities of poverty, race, sex, and homophobia; the rate of AIDS incidence among Latinos is three times that of whites, among African Americans seven times that of whites. These groups are last in line for the delivery of new treatments and the least likely to be noticed by those for whom AIDS is a thing of the past. And because their patterns of risk are shaped by the hierarchy of respectability in the first place, they are doubly jeopardized when—as is the trend in many states—policies of punitive moralism take the place of practical prevention efforts. For queer men of all races, many of the minimal prevention efforts that were formerly in place have vanished, as public and private funding evaporate in response to media coverage of treatment breakthroughs, and as the coverage produces new forms of risk by convincing people that AIDS is over. The culture of safer sex, which was built in resistance to public policy in the beginning, is now in danger of collapsing entirely.

Most people, I believe, have no idea how much a barbaric pseudo-morality continues to hamper HIV prevention, or how badly American prevention efforts compare to those of other developed nations. It is true that the original Helms Amendment of 1987 (blocking public money from any program that might "promote or encourage, directly or indirectly, homosexual sexual activity") was later replaced by slightly milder language written by Ted Kennedy. But the new version still refused funds to organizations that "promote, disseminate, or produce materials that are obscene or that depict or describe, in a patently offensive way, sexual or excretory activities or organs, including but not limited to obscene depictions of sadomasochism, homo-eroticism, the sexual exploitation of children, or any individuals engaged in sexual intercourse." It is true, too, that the restrictions imposed by the Center for Disease Control in 1986, restricting funds to programs that "would be judged by a reasonable person to be unoffensive to most educated adults," was thrown out by a federal court in 1992. But content restrictions remain in place, and although the Clinton administration initially indicated some willingness to ease them, the 1994 elections effectively ended displays of courage by the president on AIDS. New infections occur in the United States at a rate of forty thousand to eighty thousand per year. Many of these new infections are preventable: needle exchange, condom distribution, and explicitly targeted education programs have been proven effective. All continue to be blocked by law, at both federal and local levels.

The prohibition against sexiness in HIV prevention is so powerful that people take it for granted, forgetting that it is even there. To notice its grip on American culture you must first spend some time in a place where they take HIV prevention seriously, like Amsterdam or Sydney. There—by the roadside, at bus stations, in bars—you will see explicit, thoughtful, and attention-getting campaigns about HIV, other sexually transmitted diseases, and sexual health in general.

Many of them are targeted to gay men, and they don't mince words. They don't fall back on the vague euphemisms of American campaigns ("Be Careful"); they don't simply command people to use condoms; and they don't rely on fear. Many of the campaigns offer ways of thinking about real situations, such as conversations that gay couples might have about serostatus, gray areas of risk like sex between HIV-positive men, or ways of thinking about alcohol and recreational drugs that are based on acknowledgement rather than denial or prohibition. Because these publicly financed campaigns address men who have sex with men, they do not give the sense one has in the United States of implacable hostility between a national public and gay culture. Together with the widespread availability and visibility of free condoms, they sustain a general consciousness of safer sex as the standard of common practice.

None of this is true in the United States. Publicly funded campaigns are scarce, vague, and ineffective. To walk around the streets or to consult the media, one would be hard pressed to find any indication that safer sex is commonly practiced. Who could be surprised, under these conditions, to find that condoms are either absent from daily consciousness or seem obscurely passé? Most gay venues have discarded their safer sex posters. Not one of the principal gay bars in New York City still offers the bowls of condoms that used to sit on the bar or by the door. Until three years ago the Health Department provided $700,000 to $800,000 a year to Gay Men's Health Crisis for HIV prevention, and GMHC routinely placed free condoms in gay venues. The city's subsidy for prevention has been cut to $150,000, of which a mere $5,000 is allocated for condoms. In 1997 the health department in a city with 8 million residents distributed only 49,000 condoms, of which a third went to gay organizations.

Neither private organizations nor the commercial bars have filled the gap.

Quite the contrary: as people think less and less about prevention or about AIDS, their donations to private groups shrivel. At a time when charitable grant making in general has grown to record levels ($19.46 billion in 1998), philanthropic support for AIDS prevention, research, and treatment has been declining. The trend began in 1996, when protease inhibitors first became widely available, though there had been earlier signs of exhaustion with the crisis mode of AIDS activism. In 1996–97, total private support fell from $37 million to $30 million, and by 1999 groups such as GMHC were cutting personnel and programs formerly considered essential.

The effect of such changes on the front lines of the fight against HIV/AIDS is difficult to determine. From the beginning of the epidemic, all levels of government have been and continue to be reluctant to fund research into infection trends, risk, and prevention. The CDC publishes figures for diagnoses of AIDS and AIDS-related deaths, but initial infections have never been monitored in the same way. The now notorious *Sex in America* survey—the main burden of which was to convince Americans of their own normalcy—was initially conceived as research to help AIDS prevention; after its funding was gutted by congressional Republicans who feared a new Kinsey Report, the study was so reduced that it finally interviewed fewer than fifty gay men. As of June 1992, 85 percent of California's AIDS cases were classified as men who have sex with men. Yet men who have sex with men were targeted by less than 9 percent of the state's prevention money from 1991 to 1993. In New York, the figures are different because injection drug cases have outnumbered men who have sex with men every year since 1989. Still, the state's AIDS Institute issued 160 prevention contracts for the year ending June 1994; only 16 targeted men who have sex with men. Some local governments, such as San Francisco's, have tried to fill the gap. In others, such as New York City, very little has been done to find out what gay men are actually doing or how widespread HIV might be.

Yet when it comes to moralistic programs, the government has no shortage of cash. Perhaps the most dramatic example of skewed prevention priorities is buried in the Temporary Assistance to Needy Families Act, better known as "welfare reform," signed into law by President Clinton in August of 1996. A little-noticed provision—never debated in Congress or by the public before it became law—allocates $50 million dollars in federal matching funds for state dollars, for every year through 2002, targeted for "abstinence education." When combined with the state funds, this means $88 million a year, nearly half a billion dollars over the term of the law— a sum that dwarfs all other spending on HIV prevention. Essentially, we are paying the government to tell us not to have sex, and then we are calling that prevention.

The law that mandated these programs is a curious text. It defines "abstinence education" as a program exclusively devoted to "teaching the social, psychological, and health gains to be realized by abstaining from sexual activity." There is no attempt to spell out what those gains are. It is simply assumed that abstaining from sex is better. In an astonishing moment of circular reasoning, the law tells states to teach "that a mutually faithful monagamous relationship in the context of marriage is the expected standard of human sexual activity." No one is supposed to ask, "Expected by whom?"; let alone "Expected *for* whom?" (Remember, too, that this bill was supported by the likes of Congressmen Robert Livingston and Henry Hyde, and that it was signed by Bill Clinton—all of whom are willing to moralize despite their own adulteries.) Marriage is normative because it is normative; and for that reason and no other reason it is supposed to lead to physical health. The law stipulates that all qualifying programs teach "that sexual activity outside of the context marriage is likely to have harmful psychological and physical effects." How's that? How exactly does the state institution of marriage alter the *physical* effects of sex?

The nearest approach to an explanation in the bill is a clause requiring funded programs to teach "that abstinence from sexual activity is the only certain way to avoid out-of-wedlock pregnancy, sexually transmitted diseases, and other associated health problems." Apparently this passes for common sense in Washington. Other ways of avoiding pregnancy are also certain—including oral sex, anal sex, and masturbation. Many kinds of sex outside marriage will be equally safe from viral transmission, while marriage is no guarantee against HIV. The legislation is not intended to give people more options for reducing disease or pregnancy (conditions it treats as equivalent, probably because it was written with "welfare queens" in mind). The law does not even allow for the desirability of some pregnancies out of wedlock, nor for the undesirability of some pregnancies in wedlock. It is intended to stop sex and enforce monogamy, period.

The authors of the bill pretend that these measures will further the prevention of sexually transmitted diseases. In fact the opposite is true. You cannot base a realistic prevention strategy on prohibition and marriage for anyone, and especially not for men who have sex with men. Everyone even remotely connected with prevention work knows this, but policy makers still pretend otherwise, just as they did at the beginning of the crisis under Reagan. People have died and will die from AIDS because policy makers only care about

preventing HIV infection if it means preventing sex unsanc-
tioned by them. And although under Reagan a massive upsurge of activism created a culture of safer sex despite such
policies, now the alternatives to state moralism have eroded.
No one in Congress or the Clinton administration seems to
have noticed that an abstinence-only-until-marriage philosophy heavily funded by the United States is an appalling insult
to gay men and lesbians among others; and the worst part is
that because many gay men and lesbians have been convinced that the solution is same-sex marriage, they need not
worry about the disappearance of safer sex from public consciousness.

Only California and New Hampshire opted out of the abstinence program. Different states have found different uses
for the money, some better than others; programs that help
teenage girls think with greater autonomy about their life-
planning options, for example, are among the best. Insofar as
they emphasize *options,* however, they violate both the letter
and the spirit of the legislation, which is designed solely to
promote abstinence. The architects of the policy guidelines
were explicit on this point: "Sex should be confined to married couples," they said; "That both the practices and standards in many communities across the country clash with the
standard required by the law is precisely the point." And although the legislators and the president who signed the bill
appear not to have thought about the consequences for HIV
prevention, that is in itself typical of the policy environment
on prevention. The architects of the law were quite clear on
one point: they intended it as a way of taking power away
from public health officials, whom they considered too lenient on birth control, abortion, and safer sex.

Other measures that look more sympathetic to the ends of
public health prove to be no better for preventing HIV. The

same state and local governments that have done so little to deliver services to affected populations are now rushing to pass laws that look like tough action to fight the spread of the virus, but on examination turn out to be ways of punishing people who already have the virus. Unlike abstinence-only programs, many of these measures come with a public health imprimatur: in early 1999, the Centers for Disease Control and Prevention proposed national guidelines urging all fifty states to adopt HIV-reporting systems. Under CDC guidelines, doctors, labs, clinics, and blood banks would report the name and address of any person who tests positive for HIV. Local health department officials or physicians for HIV patients would also be required to do what is called contact tracing—notifying in person anyone who may have had sex or shared needles with someone with HIV. A number of states have already started such programs, and although some (such as California) report HIV cases by anonymous tracing numbers, others (such as New York, where AIDS activists might have been expected to have some voice) report by name and trace sexual contacts. Several states have passed laws criminalizing the transmission of HIV. Bills have been introduced to institute mandatory HIV testing, to allow disclosure of HIV status without consent, and to repeal antidiscrimination laws covering people with HIV/AIDS.

The rationale for many of these bills is that they are supposed to help keep track of the epidemic. The problem is that names reporting leads to faulty data. New Jersey, for example, has had a mandatory name reporting system in place since 1992, but the number of HIV cases reported there is less than one-third of the CDC's own conservative estimates. There are simple reasons for this: most HIV testing is still voluntary, and should be. Any system of voluntary testing will undercount and will be skewed by self-selection. And when people know that their names will be reported to a government agency, or when they know that their sexual partners will be contacted by case workers if they test positive, they are much less likely to be tested in the first place. Anonymous testing—one of the central strategies of the '80s, designed to encourage people to get tested for their own benefit and without danger—is now harder and harder to find. If states or the CDC really wanted to know more about rates of HIV infection without terrorizing affected people, it could turn to other means, such as blinded seroprevalence studies and statistical sampling. These alternatives remain unused, and tried-and-true methods of community prevention face shrinking funding.

Behind the paternalism of the currently fashionable surveillance techniques lies a politics that is not hard to see. Marginalized groups historically have had good reason to mistrust the government and the enthusiasm of medical experts for protecting them. Gay men of all races, undocumented immigrants, the poor, and many people of color, are not likely to trust reassurances about confidentiality—especially when twenty-nine states have laws criminalizing the sexual activity of people with HIV and each year sees added pressure to use HIV-surveillance data for more punitive measures.

Advocates of mandatory testing, names reporting, and contact tracing often cite another rationale: that with the advent of protease inhibitors, it is more important than ever to identify HIV infections early so as to deliver life-saving treatments. And so it is. But the legislators who propose these measures have failed to follow them up with programs or funding to deliver the drugs and services that are supposedly the reason for identifying new infections. Representative Tom Coburn (R—Oklahoma), for example, sponsored a bill in

1997 that he called the HIV Prevention Act. (The Coburn bill died in Congress, but some of its measures have been adopted at the state level.) It would have established centralized reporting of HIV infections, state-based partner-notification programs, and testing for HIV without consent. Coburn is also a doctor who specialized in family practice before his election to Congress, and he justified his bill as a way of delivering treatment to those who needed it. It is hard to see how anyone could swallow such an argument. The bill, which would have imposed extremely expensive new measures on a public health system that is already severely underfunded, provided neither the funds to pay for those measures nor funds to deliver the combination therapies.

Protease inhibitors are among the most expensive drugs on the market and among the most difficult to take without adequate support systems and health counseling. For the populations most affected by HIV, they remain virtually inaccessible or difficult to sustain. (This is a major reason why the demographics of AIDS is becoming increasingly marked by divisions of poverty and race; those who can pay for health care, in a nation where health care is based on wealth, have managed to control the virus better.) No new data are required to see how helpful it would be to deliver these means of secondary prevention, nor to see how important it is for primary prevention to consider the perceptions and worries of people who are considering testing. In the absence of universal health care, aggressive support systems, and targeted primary prevention, the public-health rationale of the new laws is little better than a lie.

As with abstinence-only programs, I suspect that most people on the street associate such backward-looking measures with the early days of the epidemic, before AIDS activists successfully fought for a more community-based approach to prevention. In fact, the number of these punitive measures passing state legislatures has been rising sharply each year for the past three years. As the new treatments quiet the concerns of those who can afford access to them, AIDS activism loses muscle and money, and HIV/AIDS becomes a disease of the margin that can be policed rather than treated.

Meanwhile, the straight press, learning of the continuing danger of unsafe sex, has been eager to pin the rap on gay men. The press has always loved to interpret gay men's desires as pathological: *you're on drugs, you have a tragic shortage of self-esteem, you've given up, you're irresponsible.* And for gay writers there is no easier way to get a byline in the tabloids than to scapegoat queer sex, as Randy Shilts and Larry Kramer proved the first time around. In 1994 Duncan Osborne in the *Daily News* again called for someone—Giuliani? ACT UP?—to "close the clubs, bathhouses, and porn theaters that allow their clients to have unsafe sex." *Newsday* columnist Gabriel Rotello has described sex clubs as "the killing fields of AIDS." And the *News* has drawn a touching moral from the prevention crisis: that it is time for gay men to promote "love and meaningful relationships, instead of backroom dalliances."

Not a single study has shown that a new wave of infections can be traced to sex clubs. Most risk happens in the bedroom, not the back room. One Australian study of unsafe sex among young men found that more than 70 percent of these incidents had taken place at home, with public parks and toilets at about 10 percent. In the San Francisco study of unsafe sex from 1984 to 1988, researchers asked men what their reasons had been for taking risk. Most said simply that they had been turned on. Many said that they had been "in love"—precisely what the *Daily News* recommends. Researchers have found a wide range of explanations for risk;

and sometimes they have found that there was just no explanation. In the recent study of younger men in San Francisco, seroprevalence was slightly *higher* than the overall rate among those who report that their only partner in previous twelve months was their "special relationship." The authors of that study conclude that "some of the strongest barriers to practicing safe sex may exist in close relationships where issues of intimacy, trust, and sharing risk may work against safe sex behaviors."

How ironic, then, that those who push for a more punitive approach to HIV prevention, urging measures designed to shut down sexual culture, often represent their cause as that of public health. They would have us believe that the only people arguing for maintaining a culture of safer-sex practice are antiquated libertarians. In fact, their crusade against sex reflects the dynamics of stigma and ambivalence that we saw in chapter 1. Careful reflection on public health has led most people who work in HIV prevention to conclude that an accessible sexual culture is a resource, not an enemy. If you tell gay men simply not to have sex—as the abstinence-only-until-marriage programs do—then you are merely creating a climate of alienation that furthers risk.

Closing bathhouses and sex clubs sounds like a satisfying solution. It gives the sense of identifying the problem, just by shining a flashlight on someone who's giving a blow job. *There's the enemy. Get him!* Public sexual culture has to be a resource, not a scapegoat. If we turn the shaping of that culture over to city officials and tabloid dailies and state health codes like New York's that do not even recognize the existence of safer sex, and then pat ourselves on the back for our "activism," we will have failed the challenge.

The problem is not that people have the opportunity for unsafe sex, but that they have the desire and the secret will

for it. No amount of policing is going to take away the opportunity. You can have unsafe sex in any number of bedrooms,
where there's no danger of a monitor's flashlight or Giuliani's
cops. If cubicle doors in bathhouses are "inherently unsafe,"
as Gabriel Rotello has claimed, so are bedroom doors. If you
want the city to kick down the doors to bathhouse cubicles,
but not to bedrooms, then you have focused on public sex
rather than on unsafe sex. The only way to solve the bathhouse problem, since it is also a bedroom problem, is to confront the desire and secret will for unsafe sex. If we focus on
taking away the public opportunities, we not only set ourselves a hopeless task, we distract ourselves from this harder
problem.

The campaign against public sex has nothing to do with
solving the problem of motives. I think that is exactly why
people find it attractive. The real challenge is to find an activism that will do the first job of prevention: not taking opportunities away, but giving people the resources to clarify
their own motives and to keep themselves safe rather than relying on the health department to do it for them. This means
confronting the dynamics of shame not only at the level of
public policy, where it produces measures designed to stigmatize those whose lives expose them to risk of HIV, but also
at the level of individual life itself, where shame and stigma
are often among the most intractable dimensions of risk.

THE CYCLE OF SHAME AND RISK

Those who want to clean up sex, like those who want merely
to celebrate it, commonly forget that sexiness cannot be di-
vorced from things that we really dislike about sex: irrationality, impulse, shamefulness, disgust. To this list we should
add: risk. Efforts at HIV prevention easily get tangled in con-

tradition when they try to eliminate risk and irrationality from the very activity that most stands for these dimensions of humanity. They do this most when they are most convinced that common sense and self-preservation will keep people safe.

Prevention researchers have often noted that when they survey men who have sex with men about the levels of risk in their sexual lives, the numbers never add up: far more men admit to fucking other men without condoms than admit to being fucked. Even quite aggressively "out" gay men often suffer from an intense form of what might be called "bottom shame." Their masculinity is more closely identified with insertive than with receptive anal sex. They may be lying about it, they may be allowing themselves to forget, they may be finding ways of not classifying the sex they have as getting fucked. Worse, though, is that the same sense of bottom shame is probably motivating the risk itself as well as the cover-up. Getting fucked is both clouded and intensified by shame. This leads both to a greater appeal for risk and a great incentive to deny that it has taken place, to shove the attraction from consciousness, or even to identify both risk and receptive sex with the transgression of a masculine self-image whose phoniness invited transgression in the first place.

Gay men are so aware of the language of responsibility, guilt, and shame—remember homophobia?—that they go to great lengths to avoid it. Richard Elovich, until recently director of prevention at GMHC and one of many activists who have worked hard to seek strategies more rooted in the lives of people at risk, thinks this need to avoid shame may be one reason for the link between unsafe sex and what is euphemistically called "substance use." "When people get high and have unprotected sex," he asks, "which comes first? People assume that drugs lead to unsafe sex. But often the desire is there from the beginning. Men get high or drunk because they can't acknowledge that desire, or because they want someone else to be in control, or because they just don't want to make a choice." Call it the poppers effect: you give yourself a chance to swoon. Talking dirty and going to sex clubs may work the same way. Without exactly causing unsafe sex, they may be contexts that men seek in order to escape their own self-monitoring.

The appeal of queer sex, for many, lies in its ability to shed the responsibilizing frames of good, right-thinking people. AIDS education, in contrast, until recently often called for people to feel good, affirm life, and see sex as a healthy expression of respect and self-esteem. One campaign from the San Francisco AIDS Foundation urged men to treat sex the way you might treat municipal bonds: "Playing it safe, making a plan, and sticking to it." Even the Sisters of Perpetual Indulgence, those drag activists who might seem to be the opposite extreme from the Log Cabin Club, could imagine nothing more transgressive in their safer sex book *Get the Rubber Habit* than the old gag of condoms on vegetables. Most efforts to encourage us to take care of ourselves through safer sex also encouraged us to pretend that we were never abject, or that our only desire was to be proper and good.

The queerness that is repressed in this view may be finding expression in risk. Sex has long been associated with death, in part because of its sublimity. There is no sublimity without danger, without the scary ability to imagine ourselves and everything we hold dear, at least for a moment, as relatively valueless. In this context, the pursuit of dangerous sex is not as simple as mere thrill seeking or self-destructiveness. In many cases it may represent deep and mostly unconscious thinking, about desire and the conditions that make life a value.

Critic and activist Douglas Crimp believes that, for these reasons, the emphasis on self-esteem, which many are promoting on the model of twelve-step programs, may be counterproductive: "Most people only have pop psychology for thinking about sex. Only if you can acknowledge that you have an unconscious can you admit doing self-destructive things without just feeling guilty. We all fail to realize how powerful the unconscious is. The trouble with the pop psychology of self-esteem is that it's your self that wants the risk."

In the late 1990s a number of journalists, gay and straight, have discovered some sensational appeal in the number of on-line ads that declare a desire for "bareback," or "skin-to-skin" sex. Much of the bareback trend, if it even is much of a trend, seems to be among positive men for whom the possibility of reinfection is either too speculative or too remote to outweigh the appeal of condomless sex. In the United States next to nothing has been done to give these men any real and nonjudgmental information about the evidence of reinfection, the infectivity of people whose viral load is "undetectable," or the real hazards of drug-resistant HIV. A number of negative or untested men also seem to be barebacking with any partners, even partners known to be positive, despite the risk of infection.

What is to be done about this? Well, here's one option: we could get really shocked and talk about how horrifying it is. This wouldn't do anything for the poor fuckers at risk, of course, but as long as you're talking about how scandalous and outrageous it is that some guys are having unsafe sex, you can always say you're doing your part for prevention. You, at least, are taking a moral stand. Unlike *some* people.

Some journalists would have us believe that a "core set" of wantons have chosen to "defy safer sex practice," as Michelangelo Signorile puts it in *Out*. They're endangering "the rest of us." But this shock rhetoric is pretty far removed from the lives of people at risk.

An HIV-positive friend of mine, active in HIV prevention, told me a story about a recent trick. "He took my dick in his hand and said, 'I want you to fuck me.' I said I should go get a condom," my friend continued, "and he said, 'No, don't.' When I started to get a condom anyway he said, 'I want you to fuck me without a condom.'"

Are you horrified? Wait: it gets better.

"When this has come up before with other tricks," my friend says, "I've always discussed my status, and although once or twice the other guy said it was a problem, all the other times the guy was positive and willing to take whatever risk there might be. This guy had been pretty explicit about wanting it. Still, when I was about to cum I started to pull out. He looked me in the eye and said, 'No, I want your cum.' And then afterward he said, 'And anyway I get tested every six months, and you're negative, too, right?'"

One way or another, whether he's negative or positive, my friend's trick is deluding himself about the risk he's nevertheless finding himself needing to take. Either way, he can't seem to think clearly about his own desires because they are clouded in shame and misrecognition. Will scolding solve that problem?

The same friend has another story, about a negative man who said he had been getting fucked raw by positive men. "I don't really care anymore," he explained. "Is that true?" asked my friend. "Well, no," he responded; "not really."

This guy isn't just indecisive, any more than the first one was being truly deliberate. Both are wracked with shame, despair, and conflict. We all have contradictory desires: to be safe and to be at risk; to be responsible and to fuck the law; to know what we're doing and to forget ourselves. These desires aren't equally voiced. Many are shoved from consciousness. And no amount of moralizing will solve that problem.

In fact, because of the potent strain of moralism that has distorted HIV prevention in the United States from the beginning and continues to do so, many queer men are drawn into rebelling against prevention. And for some at the extremes of the barebacking subculture, that has become the meaning of unprotected sex. This didn't have to be the case. In countries where HIV prevention has been more sensibly attuned to the dangers of shame, thinking about contexts in which condomless sex might be a tolerable risk has been the task of prevention activists, not of those in ill-considered rebellion against prevention. Australian prevention workers, for example, pioneered a set of principles for couples who, after being tested and discussing both the hazards and the terms of their trust and communication, could agree to have unprotected sex within the relationship and protected sex outside it. Canadian activists, similarly, have distributed materials to help positive men think about both the rewards and the potential risks of reinfection in condomless sex with other positive men, and also to think about ethical questions of disclosure and protection with men whose serostatus is not known to them.

For many negative men, already burned out on condoms, risk of infection seems more abstract than ever; after all, we don't see as many funerals these days. And consciously or not, people may be figuring that if they get infected, they can always go on the drugs. They probably have no experience of side effects like the Ritonavir Runs; they haven't imagined a lifetime of pills; nor does it seem real to them that they might get a resistant strain of the virus; and they probably haven't thought about living under the specter of resistance even if the drugs work at first.

At this point, of course, AIDS will strike many people as not much of a crisis. That's just it: AIDS *isn't* always a crisis. Most of the time, it has to be normal life. A crisis is a turning point, a moment of imminent change for better or worse, a moment of decision. (The root is the Greek verb for *to decide;* hence "critic" as well as "crisis.") Testing positive is a crisis, and so is getting sick. For positive people it's often the asymptomatic normal life—without crisis—that gets hard. And being negative, if your cohort has HIV and your idea of ordinary human life involves sex, means living around, under, and next to crisis for the indefinite, rest-of-your-life, blank stretch of time that you can't imagine telling a story about. You can't even say what it is that you do, exactly; there's no verb for the opposite of *seroconvert.* (Seropersist?)

Under these conditions, scaring people away from risk doesn't work. Fear is a short-term motivator, and over the long term lends sublimity to risk. Prohibitions on sex don't work either, since it is inhumane to mandate asexual life for anyone, let alone for queers, for whom sexual culture is a principal mode of sociability and public world making. Prevention has to start by imagining a mode of life that seems livable, and in which decisions about how much risk can be tolerated will not be distorted by shame and stigma. For some this may mean a stronger gay identity; but for others quite the opposite. Effective prevention, in other words, to some degree requires everyone to act as her own philosopher. "The safest way not to get HIV," says Walt Odets, author of *In the Shadow of the Epidemic,* "is never to touch another human being. So if someone is anxious, start there. But then you have to ask: what do you want to do? How important is it to you? Who are you? What do you want your life to be about?" It is time for prevention policy that tries not to answer such questions, but to provoke them.

Here we are back to the question of sexual autonomy where we began. Rather than specifying the form that other people's sex should take, or reinforcing hierarchies of shame and stigma, or pretending that those hierarchies do not exist, the best work in HIV prevention begins by acknowledging the unpredictability of sexual variance and working toward a world in which people could live sexual lives as part of a shared world. Prevention activism of this kind attempts to do the one thing that public policy has always tried to ban, even when policy makers have known that lives would be lost in the process: *promote* queer sexual culture.

Gay men cannot be expected to eliminate their unconscious. They cannot be expected to live asexual lives, or to marry as a bribe to moralists who will consider them worthy of care only on that condition. They cannot be expected individually or en masse to escape such deeply rooted cultural pathologies as male incommunicativeness, bourgeois propriety, or bottom shame. They cannot be expected to be sexual without at least some dimension of risk. They cannot be expected to follow safer sex guidelines except as people belonging to a publicly accessible culture of safer sex. They cannot be expected to sustain such a culture into the third decade of AIDS and beyond when neither public authorities nor many gay moralists are willing to acknowledge that safer sex exists or that anyone needs it. It is time not only for passive recognition of the reality of sex and risk, and not just for toleration of gay men on condition that they behave themselves, but for an actively funded and committed campaign of HIV prevention of a kind that has never been tried in the United States: one that with full public resources combats isolation, shame, and stigma rather than sex.

NOTES

Chapter One: The Ethics of Sexual Shame

2 "There is a big secret about sex: most people don't like it": Leo Bersani, "Is the Rectum a Grave?" *October* 43 (Winter 1987): 197–222, quote at page 197.

3 a sin "that perverts and extinguishes nature": quoted in Stephen Nissenbaum, *Sex, Diet, and Debility in Jacksonian America* (1980; repr. Chicago: Dorsey Press, 1988), p. 29.

10 masturbating over photos of construction workers: F. Whitam, M. Diamond, and J. Martin, "Homosexual Orientation in Twins: A Report of 61 Pairs and Three Triplet Sets," *Archives of Sexual Behavior* 22 (1993): 187–206.

13 defendants on other charges are often given tougher sentences by means of such statutes: On this and related issues in the laws of the states, see Richard Posner and Katharine Silbaugh, *A Guide to America's Sex Laws* (Chicago: Univ. of Chicago Press, 1996), pp. 98–99.

15 "nothing to do with the college's undergraduate mission": Quoted in Stanley Fish's excellent editorial, "School for the Scandalous," *New York Times*, November 21, 1997. I here agree with Fish's criticism of the free-speech defense, though I go further than he does in urging the testing of shame.

15 "the sex organs as essentially a complicated piece of plumb-

ing": quoted in Ethan Bronner, "Study of Sex on College Campuses Experiencing a Second Revolution," *New York Times*, December 28, 1997.

22 "whatever is different about it still causes allergic reactions": Theodor Adorno, "Sexual Taboos and the Law Today," in *Critical Models*, trans. Henry Pickford (New York: Columbia Univ. Press, 1998), pp. 72–73.

25 "menaces to health and safety, women and children, national security, the family, or civilization itself": Gayle Rubin, "Thinking Sex: Notes for a Radical Theory of the Politics of Sexuality," in Carole S. Vance, ed., *Pleasure and Danger: Exploring Female Sexuality* (1984; reprint, London: Pandora, 1992), pp. 267–319; quote at p. 297.

28 "spoiled identity": Erving Goffman, *Stigma: Notes on the Management of Spoiled Identity* (1963; reprint, New York: Touchstone, 1986), pp. 107–8.

28 "It became possible to suffer stigma as a homosexual quite apart from any sexual acts." This dramatic change was first emphasized by Michel Foucault, *The History of Sexuality*, vol. 1, trans. Robert Hurley (New York: Random House, 1978).

30 under which military discharges for homosexuality have skyrocketed: see Janet Halley, *Don't: A Guide to Military Antigay Policy* (Durham: Duke Univ. Press, 1999).

30 "he can neither embrace his group nor let it go": Goffman, 108.

32 "to clean up the conduct of others in the group": Goffman, 108.

33 "to be written about, not as cocks and cunts, but as *gays*": Larry Kramer, "Sex and Sensibility," *The Advocate*, May 27, 1997.

36 Dignity in the latter sense is not pomp and distinction; it is inherent in the human: See Peter Berger, "On the Obsolescence of the Concept of Honour," in Stanley Hauerwas and Alasdair MacIntyre, eds., *Revisions: Changing Perspectives in Moral Philosophy* (Notre Dame: Univ. of Notre Dame Press, 1983), pp. 172–81.

37 Subjectively, they feel nothing of the normalcy that might be attributed to them: I am indebted here to Eve Sedgwick's eloquent and indispensable essay "Queer and Now," in her *Tendencies* (Durham: Duke Univ. Press, 1993), pp. 1–20, especially pp. 5–9.

38 the fastest-selling video ever at San Francisco's principal sex-toy store, Good Vibrations: Debbie Nathan, "Sodomy for the Masses," *The Nation*, April 19, 1999.

Chapter Two: What's Wrong with Normal?

42 "I want to be able to show her a magazine." Quoted in Wayne Hoffman, "No Sex Please! We're Gay," *New York Blade*, June 24, 1998.

46 His 1953 article about the stigma he felt from the arrest: Dale Jennings, "To Be Accused, Is to Be Guilty," *One*, January 1953, 10–13; reprinted in Mark Blasius and Shane Phelan, *We Are Everywhere: A Historical Sourcebook of Gay and Lesbian Politics* (New York: Routledge, 1997), pp. 310–12.

46 "irrelevant to our ideals, our principles, our hopes and aspirations": These details come from the excellent account in John D'Emilio, *Sexual Politics, Sexual Communities: The Making of a Homosexual Minority in the United States, 1940–1970* (Chicago: Univ. of Chicago Press, 1983). Some of the key documents are reprinted in Blasius and Phelan, *We Are Everywhere*.

54 "people who belong to the statistical majority feel superior to those who do not": Mary Poovey, "Sex in America," *Critical Inquiry* 24.2 (Winter 1998): 366–92, at p. 374.

55 "when they call for a clean-up of the sex offenders in a community": Alfred C. Kinsey, et al., *Sexual Behavior in the Human Male* (Philadelphia: W. B. Saunders, 1948), p. 392.

56 "how much man, without his knowledge, is subject to divine laws and with what regularity he realizes them": Georges Canguilhem, *The Normal and the Pathological*, trans. Carolyn Fawcett (New York: Zone Books, 1991), p. 158. The first part of Canguilhem's book was published in 1943, as *Essay on Some Problems Concerning the Normal and the Pathological*. Canguilhem simplified the title for the much expanded version he published in 1966.

61 "Following legalization of same-sex marriage . . . close down the gay rights movement for good": quoted in David Groff, ed., *Out Facts: Just about Everything You Need to Know about Gay and Lesbian Life* (New York: Universe, 1997).

64 "I called for a new post-gay identity . . .": this and subsequent

quotes from James Collard are in "Leaving the Gay Ghetto," *Newsweek*, August 17, 1998.

71–72 "two major forces that have roiled" . . . "who want to throw rocks through the window": Adam Nagourney, "Gay Politics and Anti-Politics: A Movement Divided," *New York Times*, October 25, 1998.

77 At about the same time, the national organizations realigned themselves: Urvashi Vaid, who witnessed many of these developments from the inside in her years of working at the National Gay and Lesbian Task Force, wrote insightfully about the realignment of the 1990s in her 1995 book *Virtual Equality: The Mainstreaming of Gay and Lesbian Liberation* (New York: Doubleday, 1995).

Chapter Three: Beyond Gay Marriage

81 "The institution of marriage is trivialized by same-sex marriage": The exchange of May 30, 1996, is reproduced in Andrew Sullivan, ed., *Same-Sex Marriage: Pro and Con* (New York: Vintage, 1997), pp. 225–26.

83 What purpose could be served by a skeptical discussion of marriage now, given the nature of the opposition? Jesse Helms's speech on the Senate floor in favor of the Defense of Marriage Act is printed in Robert M. Baird and Stuart E. Rosenbaum, eds., *Same-Sex Marriage: The Moral and Legal Debate* (Amherst: Prometheus Books, 1997), p. 22. Jean Bethke Elshtain's "Against Gay Marriage" appeared in *Commonweal*, October 22, 1991, and is reprinted in Andrew Sullivan, ed., *Same-Sex Marriage: Pro and Con: A Reader* (New York: Vintage, 1997), pp. 57–60. Pope John Paul II is quoted by the *New York Times*, "Pope Deplores Gay Marriage," February 23, 1994.

83 "The ship has sailed": Evan Wolfson, "Crossing the Threshold: Equal Marriage Rights for Lesbians and Gay Men, and the Intra-Community Critique," *New York University Review of Law and Social Change* 21 (1994): 567–615, p. 611. See also Evan Wolfson, "Why We Should Fight for the Freedom to Marry," *Journal of Gay, Lesbian, and Bisexual Identity* 1 (Jan. 1996).

90 "repeal of all legislative provisions . . . victimizing single persons and same-sex couples": quoted in William Eskridge, *The Case for Same-Sex Marriage: From Sexual Liberty to Civilized Commitment* (New York: The Free Press, 1996), p. 54.

91 "Among some gays . . . enemy of more desirable institutions":
Robert M. Baird and Stuart E. Rosenbaum, eds., *Same-Sex Marriage:
The Moral and Legal Debate* (Amherst: Prometheus Books, 1997), pp.
10–11.

92 "to the extent that same-sex marriage might embolden some
couples . . . would seem almost irrelevant": Eskridge, *The Case for
Same-Sex Marriage: From Sexual Liberty to Civilized Commitment* (New
York: The Free Press, 1996), p. 82.

93 "Whatever gravity gay life may have lacked . . . the value of a
committed partner is incalculable": Eskridge, *The Case for Same-Sex
Marriage: From Sexual Liberty to Civilized Commitment* (New York: The
Free Press, 1996), pp. 58, 74.

95 the fundamental issue "is not the desirability of marriage, but
rather the desirability of the right to marry": Tom Stoddard, "Why
Gay People Should Seek the Right to Marry," *Out/Look* 6.8 (1990);
repr. in Mark Blasius and Shane Phelan, eds., *We Are Everywhere: A
Historical Sourcebook of Gay and Lesbian Politics* (New York: Routledge,
1997), quotation on p. 756.

96 "If it is freely chosen . . . the right society has never granted":
Evan Wolfson, "Crossing the Threshold," pp. 582–83.

97 "The most important unresolved question . . . can pursue
other avenues": Mary C. Dunlap, "The Lesbian and Gay Marriage Debate: A Microcosm of Our Hopes and Troubles in the Nineties," *Law
and Sexuality* 1 (1991): 63–96, p. 90.

98 "Whatever the history . . . and, for some, their religious community": Evan Wolfson, "Crossing the Threshold," p. 479.

99 "How could a feminist, out, radical lesbian like myself . . .
those who participate in my world": Barbara Cox, "A (Personal) Essay
on Same-Sex Marriage," in Baird and Rosenbaum, *Same-Sex Marriage:
The Moral and Legal Debate,* pp. 27–29. This essay was originally a
long footnote to an article in the *Wisconsin Law Review,* so the disappearance of the law and the state from Cox's understanding of marriage is especially telling.

101 "The right joining in marriage is the work of the Lord only . . . .
we are but witnesses" [Fox] and "Not felon-like law-bound, but wedded in desires" [Clare]: both quoted in Christopher Hill, *Liberty against
the Law: Some Seventeenth-Century Controversies* (London: Penguin,
1997), pp. 201–203.

104 "The suggestion that lesbians and gay men . . . the imputation seems wrong, as well as unfair": Evan Wolfson, "Crossing the Threshold," p. 585.

105 "Does everyone who gets married . . . endorse every retrograde aspect of marriage?": Evan Wolfson, "Crossing the Threshold," p. 602.

106 "My partner of the past decade is not a domestic partner . . . Marrying under such conditions is not a totally free choice": Claudia Card, "Against Marriage and Motherhood," *Hypatia* 11.3 (Summer 1996): 1–23, p. 7.

110 "If marriage is to work . . . a general norm, rather than a personal taste": Jonathan Rauch, "For Better or Worse?" *The New Republic,* May 6, 1996; repr. in Sullivan, *Same-Sex marriage, Pro and Con,* 169–81, quotation on p. 180.

110 "Marriage would provide status to those who married . . . for significant periods of time": Gabriel Rotello, "Creating a New Gay Culture: Balancing Fidelity and Freedom," *The Nation,* April 21, 1997, 11–16. See also Gabriel Rotello, *Sexual Ecology: AIDS and the Destiny of Gay Men* (New York: Dutton, 1997), p. 15.

110 Most gay advocates of marriage "are generally careful not to make the case for marriage . . . encouraging gay men and lesbians to marry": Gabriel Rotello, "Creating a New Gay Culture."

111 "If gay marriage is recognized . . . shame on us": Rauch, "For Better or Worse?" in Sullivan, *Same-Sex Desire, Pro and Con,* pp. 180–81.

111 "the puritanical impulse . . . where all sexual expression outside wedlock is morally tainted": Fenton Johnson, "Wedded to an Illusion: Do Gays and Lesbians Really Want the Right to Marry?" *Harper's,* November 1996, 43–50, p. 47.

112 "There are very few social incentives of the kind conservatives like . . . to modify and change that behavior for the better": Andrew Sullivan, *Same-Sex Marriage: Pro and Con: A Reader,* p. 168.

113 marriage as a social institution is "marked by integrity and caring . . . gay bars, pornography, and one-night stands": Bishop John Shelby Spong, "Blessing Gay and Lesbian Commitments," in Sullivan, *Same-Sex Marriage, Pro and Con,* pp. 79–80.

113 "to presume that morality follows on marriage is to ignore

centuries of evidence that each is very much possible without the other": Fenton Johnson, "Wedded to an Illusion: Do Gays and Lesbians Really Want the Right to Marry?" *Harper's,* November 1996, 43–50, p. 47.

117 "Marriage is a status rich in entitlements": Richard Posner, *Sex and Reason,* quoted in Andrew Sullivan, *Same-Sex Marriage: Pro and Con,* p. 209.

121 "Whatever the context of the debate, most speakers are transfixed by the *symbolism* of legal recognition": Eskridge devotes some space to the legal benefits, but Chambers points out that it amounts to six out of his 261 pages. David L. Chambers, "What If? The Legal Consequences of Marriage and the Legal Needs of Lesbian and Gay Male Couples," *Michigan Law Review* 95 (November 1996): 447–91, p. 450.

123 "In a common-law arrangement . . . marriage is and should be viewed as epiphenomenal or derivative—and not vice versa": Richard Mohr, "The Case for Gay Marriage," in Baird and Rosenbaum, *Same-Sex Marriage: The Moral and Legal Debate,* p. 94.

127 writes that his critics "come close to essentializing marriage as an inherently regressive institution": William Eskridge, *The Case for Same-Sex Marriage,* p. 76.

127 marriage is "socially constructed, and therefore transformable": Evan Wolfson, "Crossing the Threshold," p. 589.

131 Richard Mohr, for example, asserts . . . does not have a necessary relation to commitment or love: Richard Mohr, "The Case for Gay Marriage," p. 96.

131 David McWhirter and Andrew Mattison report . . . five years or more were: David P. McWhirter and Andrew M. Mattison, *The Male Couple: How Relationships Develop* (Englewood Cliffs: Prentice-Hall, 1984), pp. 252–59.

131 "more than one long-term intimate relationship during the same time period": Claudia Card, "Against Marriage and Motherhood," p. 8.

132 "This argument is not easily evaluated . . . the effects of legal and social innovation": Morris Kaplan, *Sexual Justice* (New York: Routledge, 1997), p. 225.

136 "It is marriage": Andrew Sullivan, "The Marriage Moment,"

The Advocate, January 20, 1998, pp. 61–63. Sullivan's dismissive joke about the queer theorist who "hilariously" remarks that "there is no orgasm without ideology"—not a bad line at all, in my view—refers to David Halperin, "Historicizing the Sexual Body: Sexual Preferences and Erotic Identities in the Pseudo-Lucianic *Erôtes,*" in Domna C. Stanton, ed., *Discourses of Sexuality: From Aristotle to AIDS* (Ann Arbor: Univ. of Michigan Press, 1992), 236–61, quotation on p. 261; also in Jan Goldstein, ed., *Foucault and the Writing of History* (Oxford: Basil Blackwell, 1994), 13–34, quotation on p. 34. The sentence reads: "If the sexual body is indeed historical—if there is, in short, no orgasm without ideology—perhaps ongoing inquiry into the politics of pleasure will serve to deepen the pleasures, as well as to widen the possibilities, of politics."

Chapter Four: Zoning Out Sex

154 evidence that there has been no "sex panic" in New York: Gabriel Rotello, editorial, *LGNY,* July 27, 1997.

163 "an influx of polluting revelers": quoted in "As Piers Close, Gay Protesters See a Paradise Lost," *New York Times,* September 14, 1997.

166 sex "dominates gay male—and now young lesbian—culture . . . it is consumeristic and ultimately hollow": *The Advocate,* Sept. 6, 1994, p. 80.

180 "the careful work of disattention": Erving Goffman, *Stigma: Notes on the Management of Spoiled Identity* (1963; repr. New York: Simon & Schuster, 1986), p. 41.

181 Americans "should have the absolute right to buy all magazines and books judged to be legal": Marcia Pally, *Sex & Sensibility: Reflections on Forbidden Mirrors and the Will to Censor* (Hopewell, NJ: Ecco Press, 1994), pp. 69–70.

184 "dead citizens": Lauren Berlant, *The Queen of America Goes to Washington City: Essays on Sex and Citizenship* (Durham: Duke University Press, 1997), passim.

188 "at least that's my perception . . . just coming out now because they feel more protected": Michelangelo Signorile, *Life Outside* (New York: Harper Collins, 1997), p. 195.

191 "The human being has the need to accumulate energies and to spend them . . . Would there not also be the need for a time for these

encounters, these exchanges?": Henri Lefebvre, *Writings on Cities,* trans. Eleonore Kofman and Elizabeth Lebas (Oxford: Blackwell, 1996), pp. 147–48.

Conclusion: The Politics of Shame and HIV Prevention.

200 "promote . . . sadomasochism, homo-eroticism, the sexual exploitation of children, or any individuals engaged in sexual intercourse": *Congressional Record,* 1st. session, 1989, v. 135, no. 134, S12967.

201 Until three years ago the Health Department . . . of which a third went to gay organizations: "AIDS Fears Rise as Gay Bars Offer Fewer Condoms," *New York Times,* April 25, 1999.

202 At a time when charitable grant making in general has grown . . . cutting personnel and programs formerly considered essential: see the 1999 report from Funders Concerned about AIDS, *Philanthropy and HIV: Assessing the Past, Shaping the Future.*

203 The law that mandated these programs is a curious text . . . too lenient on birth control, abortion, and safer sex: much of the information in these paragraphs can be found in the Sexuality Information and Education Council of the United States (SIECUS) 1999 report titled Between the Lines: States' Implementation of the Federal Government's Section 510(b) Abstinence Education Program in Fiscal Year 1998.

208 Representative Tom Coburn (R—Oklahoma) . . . justified his bill as a way of delivering treatment to those who needed it: See, for example, his remarks in "Tom Coburn Talks AIDS," *Poz,* July 1997.

214 "defy safer sex practice . . . the rest of us": Michelangelo Signorile, *Out,* June 1997.

Acknowledgments

I would like to acknowledge *GLQ* for printing a substantially different version of chapter 3. Its citation is "Normal and Normaller: Beyond Gay Marriage," *GLQ* 5.2 (199): 119–71.

I would also like to offer a personal acknowledgment to Sean Belman, who, in addition to offering thoughtful commentary, constantly showed me how much there is to be said for life out of wedlock.